Contents

Acknowledgements

There are so many people to thank for their support in writing this book it is difficult to know where to begin. I wish to express my sincere gratitude to my colleague Dr. Isabelle Brodie for her assistance with fieldwork and data analysis but especially for her enduring patience in commenting on several earlier drafts of different chapters of this manuscript. I particularly want to acknowledge the contribution of her ideas, knowledge and insights and her help with editing many sections of this text.

I am indebted to my colleague Professor John Pitts for giving his time and effort to focus my thinking; I am especially grateful for his editing suggestions, his wise counsel and extremely sound advice. Thanks are due to my sister Rosemary for assisting in the compilation of the bibliography and saving me precious time. I must thank Geoffrey Mann at Russell House Publishing for suggesting the idea of the book, and I am also grateful to SCODA for making funds for the research available. My sincere thanks go to the many hard-pressed professionals for giving their time to the project and through whose efforts access to the young people was facilitated. Finally, my biggest thanks of all go to the young people who took part. Their generosity in sharing their experiences has made the book possible and I hope that in turn I have done justice to those experiences.

Abbreviations

ACMD	Advisory Council on the Misuse of Drugs
CYT	Crucible Youth Theatre
DDU	Drug Dependency Unit
DORA	Defence of the Realm Act
DoH	Department of Health
DTTO	Drug Treatment and Testing Order
HAS	Health Advisory Council
ISDD	Institute for the Study of Drug Dependence
NAYJ	National Association for Youth Justice
PHSE	Personal, Health and Social Education
PRU	Pupil Referral Unit
SCODA	Standing Conference on Drug Abuse
SEU	Social Exclusion Unit
YOT	Youth Offending Team

Note

In order to protect their confidentiality, the names of all the young people referred to in this book have been changed.

Introduction

The subject of drugs is one that appears to inspire both fear and fascination, and in Britain in recent years, this issue has received a great deal of attention from the media, politicians, the police and others as increasing numbers of young people have become involved in drug use.

In this book, a contribution to this debate is made by discussing the involvement of some young people in drug use. These were young people who had already been identified as more likely to become involved in drug taking because they had previously:

- offended
- been excluded from, or not attended, school
- been looked after in the local authority care system

Attention was drawn to these groups because previous evidence has suggested that they, amongst other 'vulnerable' groups, are most at risk of developing problems in relation to drug use (Health Advisory Service (HAS), 1996; President of the Council 1998). Other groups who are thought to be at greater risk of initiating drug use are those who:

- are homeless
- have alcohol or drug abusing parents
- have learning difficulties
- have been sexually abused or exploited through prostitution
- have a history of family problems
- have mental health problems

(HAS, 1996; Standing Conference on Drug Abuse (SCODA), 1997)

Offending, School Exclusion and Being Looked After

Indications suggest that there are higher prevalence rates of drug use among young offenders than other groups and, although the evidence is relatively weak, that young offenders are at greater risk of developing harmful patterns of drug use (Newburn, 1999). An Audit Commission study, involving 103 young offenders on supervision orders, reported that 65 per cent had used cannabis, one quarter had used amphetamine, over one fifth had used ecstasy, just under one fifth LSD, over one tenth had used cocaine and approximately six per cent had used heroin (Audit Commission, 1996).

Although the offending careers of young people are often informal or transient, evidence suggests that young people involved in *persistent* offending tend not to 'grow out of crime' (Rutherford, 1986, cited in Pitts, 1999). This appears to be especially the case in relation to those who endure 'enforced adolescence'—that is, when young people are prevented by their social and economic conditions from assuming the responsibilities of 'adulthood', they tend to grow *into* rather than *out of* crime. Further, the intensification of their criminal involvement is 'often accompanied by much heavier drinking and drug taking' (Pitts, 2001).

In discussing young people who have been excluded from school, a broad definition of exclusion is employed to include young people who have truanted from school and who thus, to some extent, might be said to have excluded themselves (Collison, 1996). The term, 'young people who are excluded from school', also refers to those who have been temporarily or permanently removed from school as a form of punishment. The nature of the relationship between exclusion from school and substance misuse is more complex though drug related incidents are often cited as the official reason for exclusion. For example, some types of substance use may contribute to other forms of difficult behaviour that make it more likely that a young person will be excluded. OFSTED reports that while levels of exclusion for drug related incidents did not increase during 1996–7, there were known instances where pupils were excluded for reasons associated with drug use, for example, violent behaviour following the consumption of alcohol. None of the young people to whom we spoke had been excluded from school for this reason.

The term 'looked after' replaces the term 'in care' and refers to all children who are the subject of a care order, or who are provided with accommodation on a voluntary basis for more than 24 hours. Being 'looked after' may not be the way that children in the public care system would describe their experiences but nevertheless this is the term used by professionals working in this field and is therefore the term employed in this book. Children may also be looked after by way of a planned series of short-term placements. This tends to be thought of as a way in which local authorities support disabled children and their families, traditionally termed 'respite care', but in fact available statistics show that other reasons, including family stress and relationship difficulties, are equally important. On any one day, some 53,000 children are likely to be looked after by local authorities. In the course of a year, many more young people will of course move in and out of the care system. Studies of young people who are looked after have suggested that over a third of young people had been involved in substance use while being looked after. A close relationship between substance misuse and offending, amongst those who are looked after, has also been found, with almost seven in ten of those involved in substance use having offended in the past (Wade *et al.*, 1998).

We know from previous research that the disadvantages these young people experience tend to overlap. It has been shown, for example, that the risk of school exclusion is greater for young people who have been looked after and that involvement in offending is more likely when a young person has been excluded from school (Martin *et al.*, 1999). Equally, troublesome behaviour that may perhaps include offending may contribute to a young person being looked after. All these groups of young people are known to be extremely disadvantaged in terms of their family backgrounds (OFSTED, 1996; Department of Health, 1998a).

Disentangling the experiences of each of these groups, their relationships to each other and with substance misuse is therefore an extremely complex task. Professionals working with such young people are usually aware that these individuals have 'multiple' problems. Amongst the young people who took part there were very definite overlaps between the experiences of offending, being excluded from school and being looked after in the local authority care system. The original intention had been to include three groups of young people:

- Those who had offended.
- Those who had been excluded from school.
- Those who had been looked after in the local authority care system.

However, because of the degree of overlap between these experiences seven rather than three groups were identified. These are:

- Those who had offended only.
- Those who had been excluded from school only.
- Those who had been looked after only.
- Those who had offended *and* been excluded from school.
- Those who had offended, been excluded from school *and* been looked after in the local authority care system.
- Those who had been excluded from school *and* looked after in the local authority care system.
- Those who had offended *and* been looked after in the local authority care system.

49 of the young people were aged 13–18 years and 10 were 19–25 years. Many of these young people had experienced a number of difficulties in their lives and the extent to which their experiences of offending, being excluded from school and being looked after overlap is an indication of the severity of the problems they faced. Many had also experienced difficult relationships in their families and approximately half said they had experienced some form of conflict or abuse within the family. Five reported that they had been sexually abused within the family. The family difficulties they faced ranged from arguments with parents to neglect and physical or sexual abuse.

'Paul'

Paul, a seventeen-year-old who had offended, been excluded from school and looked after, had started using cannabis when he was 'about eleven'. When he was thirteen or fourteen, he began experimenting with other drugs such as amphetamine, LSD, cocaine and ecstasy. Paul became looked after when he was nine and spoke about his life before this:

P.   *My dad's been in jail most of my life and my stepfather was an alcoholic.*

Q.   *And how would you describe your relationship with your mum and dad when you lived at home?*

P.   *Bad. My mum's a paranoid schizophrenic, an' like, I was always arguing with her and my step-dad was just always steaming, so, an' like, they were always arguing with my sisters and stuff, so, just constantly arguing. It used to do my head in.*

In addition to the conflict and abuse they had encountered, many of these young people came from fairly unstable family backgrounds. Just a quarter came from nuclear families and, of the other three-quarters, almost equal proportions came from single parent households, reconstituted families and households where their parents had divorced. To add to their difficulties, approximately a quarter of the young people reported that their parents used drugs and a small group of five said that their parents drank excessively.

Although a direct cause-effect relationship is not being proposed here, it is clear that the quality of relationships within the family is important in the experience of adolescence generally, and in particular, difficult family relationships are often associated with a range of problematic behaviours in adolescence (Lloyd *et al.*, 1998; ACMD, 1998; Martin *et al.*, 1999). Research has shown that when young people come from situations of family abuse or neglect, 'the chances of developing problematic patterns of drug use are greatly increased' (McCallum, 1998). It has also been shown that such factors are important in the lives of young people who experience school exclusion (OFSTED, 1996) and several studies have suggested that they are associated with the development of later delinquency (Martin *et al.*, 1999).

Other research evidence further supports the view that those who become looked after, or who are excluded from school, tend to be at the extreme end of problematic behaviours. Schools do not make the decision to exclude lightly, nor are there many children admitted to public care who do not need to be there (Department for Education and Employment, 1999; Department for Education and Employment/Department of Health, 1999). Focusing our attention on the drug use of 'vulnerable groups' however, may lead us to forget that drug taking appears to have become a 'normal' activity for many young people (Parker *et al.*, 1998). It would be surprising, therefore, if those who are rendered the most vulnerable and disadvantaged did not also engage in drinking alcohol, smoking and the use of illicit substances (see for example, Bourgois, 1996; Pettiway, 1997). By focusing on the 'vulnerability' of these young people as offenders, young people who have been excluded from school or looked after, we should not lose sight of the fact that there are other factors in a young person's environment that put them at risk of drug use.

Understanding Adolescent Drug Use

In the past twenty years, there has been a certain neglect of studies that try to understand young people's drug use (Parker *et al.*, 1998; Merchant and MacDonald, 1994). This perhaps results from 'something in the culture of the late twentieth century' which has tended to privilege 'quantitative approaches in social science' (Pearson, 1999: p. 483). As a consequence of this tendency, it has been possible to measure the increase in drug use amongst young people but why it is happening has been insufficiently understood (Parker *et al.*, 1998).

Explanations of drug use by young people have been couched in discussions of 'risk' and 'resiliency', factors which are thought to make young people more or less 'vulnerable' to drug use. A difficult childhood temperament, lack of attachment to school and low degree of commitment to education, association with drug-using peers, attitudes favourable to use and alienation from, or rejection of, the dominant value system are thought to increase the risk that a young person will develop drug misuse problems. The young people discussed in this book experienced these risk factors.

On the other hand, an easy temperament, intellectual capabilities, self-efficacy, 'empathy' and 'humour' have been identified as 'resiliency skills' in several studies.

The Health Advisory Service (1996) has also identified 'a caring relationship with at least one adult' and 'external systems of support that encourage positive values' as important in making some young people resilient to developing drug misuse problems.

Experiences of offending, being excluded from school or being looked after in local authority care, and the processes that lead to such experiences, no doubt constitute 'negative stresses' (Norman, 1994) in the lives of young people. It might even be argued that such young people have rejected, or are alienated from, the dominant value system. The extent of drug use amongst young people who are not 'vulnerable' as a result of these experiences, however, suggests that it would be simplistic to assume a direct causal relationship between 'vulnerability' as a result of offending, being excluded from school or being looked after and drug misuse (q.v. Parker *et al.*, 1998). If 'resiliency' skills are important in reducing the likelihood that a young person will develop problems in relation to drug use, the question we need to be asking is, 'How can we encourage the development of such skills in young people who are confronted with multiple difficulties and disadvantages?'

This book aims to show that the poverty and disorganisation of the families and communities from which these young people so often come, and the failure of social institutions to provide for them adequately mitigate against the development of such skills.

These background factors also appear to put them at risk of becoming involved in offending, of being excluded from school and of 'being looked after'.

This book argues, therefore, that these three circumstances are not the sole determinants of a young person's vulnerability to drug use, but that the factors that render them vulnerable have deeper roots.

The Government's Drug Strategy

Contemporary concern about drug use by the young is so great that in 1998, the New Labour government launched its strategy, *Tackling Drugs to Build a Better Britain: The Government's Ten-year Strategy for Tackling Drugs Misuse*. The strategy has four main aims:

1. To help young people resist drugs and fulfil their potential in society.
2. To protect communities from drug-related anti-social and criminal behaviour.
3. To enable people with drug problems to overcome them and live healthy and crime-free lives.
4. To stifle the availability of drugs on the streets (President of the Council, 1998).

The new drug strategy also explicitly aims to reduce the numbers of young people reporting use of drugs such as heroin and cocaine. In terms of policy priorities, the overlap between the interests of the groups of vulnerable young people we are considering here is increasingly taken for granted. The new drug strategy, for example, specifically highlights 'vulnerable groups', and the strong links between drugs problems, exclusion or truancy from school, break-up of the family and initiation into criminal activity. It argues that there should be increased access to intervention and services for vulnerable groups, including school excludees, truants, looked after children, young offenders, young homeless people and children of drug-misusing parents. It introduces a number of new initiatives with a focus on 'joined up practice' (multi-agency approaches) in local communities and a 'drugs tsar' has been appointed co-ordinator. What is important about this new approach is that it acknowledges that drug problems do not usually occur in a vacuum but are linked to a number of other social problems such as unemployment, homelessness and material deprivation (President of the Council, 1998).

The relationship between drug use and offending has been high on the political agenda throughout the 1990s (President of the Council, 1998; Parker *et al.*, 1998; Graham and Bowling, 1995; Tyler, 1995). Problematic users, usually involving intravenous use of heroin or use of crack-cocaine, represent just a small fraction of *all* drug users but the evidence demonstrates that they are responsible for a disproportionate amount of crime, especially acquisitive crime (Edmunds *et al.*, 1998). One study found that over a three-month period, 664 drug addicts had committed 70,000 offences between them (President of the Council, 1998). Another found that in a random sample of arrestees, 60 per cent had traces of illegal drugs in their urine (Bennett, 1998).

A Home Office report has shown that very few problematic users are able to support their drug use through legal means and suggests that at least £200 may represent a realistic estimate of the UK average amount each problematic user spends each week (Edmunds *et al.*, 1998). Other studies have suggested that the weekly median spend may be between £300 and £600 per week (May *et al.*, 2000).

The new drugs strategy pursues the intention of 'breaking the link between drugs and crime' in order to 'protect communities from drug-related anti-social and criminal behaviour' (Cabinet Office, 1999). In order to do so, Drug Treatment and Testing Orders (DTTOs) have been introduced and extra money has been allocated for the development of Arrest Referral Schemes. These aim to provide 'offenders with drug problems the opportunity to tackle their drug misuse and reduce offending' (Hellawell, 1998/99).

The government has also issued guidelines in relation to managing drug-related incidents in schools and suggests that a range of responses to such incidents should be developed, 'rather than a policy of automatic permanent exclusion which may only serve to exacerbate the child's drug problems' (President of the Council, 1998). All schools are now required to have a written drug policy and to develop drug education in the Personal, Health and Social Education (PHSE) curriculum.

The Structure of the Book

Chapter One begins the discussion by attempting to clarify the concept of 'drugs'. The modern histories of some drugs are explored, particularly those in which many young people in contemporary Britain routinely indulge, and which had certainly been consumed by the young people who took part in this study. This provides a context in which to locate contemporary concerns about young people and drug use. The chapter demonstrates that concerns about drug use have been present throughout the twentieth century but that concerns about young people, particularly 'vulnerable' young people, using drugs, and the types of drug that they use, have emerged only in the latter part of that century.

In *Chapter Two*, the discussion continues with an attempt to come to terms with the concept of 'youth' and the position of young people in contemporary society. The nature of that society and the ways in which young people have been affected by social policy changes in the past twenty years are considered. In this chapter the question, of whether there is something about contemporary society that makes it more likely that young people, especially those who are vulnerable, will take drugs is raised.

Chapter Three makes the connection between the kinds of vulnerabilities discussed in earlier chapters and the risk of serious involvement in drug use. Readers are introduced to the young people by exploring their backgrounds and current living situations. The chapter clearly demonstrates the multiple disadvantages to which many of these young people are subject. The possible relationships between 'vulnerability' as a result of offending, being excluded from school or being looked after and beginning to use drugs are considered.

In *Chapter Four*, the motivations of these young people for using drugs are discussed. How the young people were introduced to drugs and how they managed to access and pay for them is also explored. The chapter shows that the reasons young people begin to use drugs are often complex and cannot be attributed to one single cause. It suggests that interventions to respond to drug use amongst the young will only be successful if their motivations for using drugs are understood. The chapter also demonstrates the significance of peer group influences in a young person's decision to use drugs and shows that the law does not seem to provide a barrier to accessing licit or illicit substances.

Chapter Five explores the patterns of drug use these young people had developed and examines the ages at which they had begun to use drugs. It shows that they had used more licit and illicit substances at younger ages than their less vulnerable peers, and had developed more worrying patterns of use. It also demonstrates, however, that many of these young people appeared just as capable as their not-so-vulnerable peers of modifying over time their behaviour in relation to drug use.

Chapter Six looks at how the young people perceived their drug use and considers the sorts of things they said about what help they might like in order to stop using drugs. The chapter shows that their views on both these counts makes the practice of working with and caring for young people who experience multiple disadvantages, and who are using drugs, all the more difficult.

Chapter Seven indicates that, amongst this group of young people, young women's drug use had overtaken that of the young men. These differences may of course be distinct to this group and may not be found amongst less troubled young people. The chapter considers what these patterns of drug consumption suggest about the relationship between gender, 'vulnerability' and drug use. This chapter argues that it is important to take account of gender differences because discussion of 'vulnerability' factors such as offending and exclusion from school have, in the past, been dominated by the experiences of young men (Collison, 1996; Parker, 1996). Consequently, we know comparatively little about the repercussions of offending, being excluded from school or being looked after in the lives of young women. Additionally, studies of drug use have also suffered from gender 'blindness' and have tended to assume that women's experiences can be understood by extrapolating from the experience of men (Henderson, 1999; Denton and O'Malley, 1999; McCallum, 1998; Maher, 1995; Ettorre, 1992; Oppenheimer, 1989; Blom and van den Berg; 1989).

In *Chapter Eight*, the final chapter, the relationship between 'vulnerability', 'social exclusion' and drug use is briefly considered. A number of government initiatives to respond to 'excluded youth' are scrutinised and the implications of the issues raised in this book for those working in a variety of practice situations with young people are discussed. It is hoped that the book will prove valuable to such professionals in many different contexts and that the insights derived from this work will deepen our understandings of *all* young people and their drug use.

Chapter 1

Licit and Illicit Drugs: The Historical Connection

Introduction

This chapter begins by taking a brief historical excursion, in an attempt to clarify the concept of 'drugs'. The language and terminology employed to discuss this subject have often served to confuse the debate (Dally, 1998). The concept of 'drugs' is historically variable (Parascandola, 1998) and based on moral and political judgements. As a concept, therefore, 'drugs' has no scientific validity (Ruggerio, 1999; Tyler, 1995); many things ordinarily encountered in everyday life, such as medicines, poisons, tea and coffee could be described as 'drugs' (South, 1999).

What Do We Mean by 'Drugs'?

So widespread is the consumption of 'drugs' like tea, coffee and alcohol in everyday life, that many normal situations are unthinkable without them. This, however, was not always the case. In seventeenth century Britain, for example, coffee houses were viewed suspiciously by King Charles II as 'hotbeds of sedition' (Matthee, 1998: p. 36) in which 'the spreading of malicious and shameful reports' was considered to harm 'the King's majesty and the realm' (Tyler, 1995: p. 131). Women were not allowed in coffee houses at this time and they tended to hold coffee responsible for causing domestic strife and making men sexually impotent (Matthee, 1998: p. 36). As a consequence of their concerns, the 'Women's Petition Against Coffee' was submitted to King Charles II. In 1675, due to the political threat that coffee houses were considered to present, rather than because of the concerns of women, the King ordered that they all be closed (Matthee, 1998: p. 36; Tyler, 1995: p. 131). As a result of popular protest, however, the measure was repealed within ten days. In the eighteenth century, tea was also condemned in certain circles because it was said to lead to idleness and allegedly had an 'effeminate aura' (Matthee, 1999: p. 35).

On the other hand, medicinal drugs such as tranquillisers, which were developed in the late 1950s, are legally available with a prescription and widely used (Robson, 1999: p. 161). In the 1980s there were between 0.25 million and 1.25 million dependent users for whom tranquillisers were legally prescribed, many of whom were women (Tyler, 1995: p. 441, Robson, 1999; South, 1997). By the 1990s these drugs were being used illegally by recreational users (Tyler 1995: p. 442) and the 'extensive' illicit market is supplied 'entirely by diversion from legal supplies' (Robson, 1999: p. 161).

In recent years, homeopathic drugs have become readily available without a prescription and are consumed extensively for a variety of conditions. When we talk about 'drugs' however, it is not normally substances such as tea and coffee, prescription drugs or homeopathic medicines to which reference is made. When it is used today, the concept is most commonly associated with illegal or illicit drugs and with 'abuse' (South, 1999; Parascandola, 1998). Illicit drugs are usually differentiated from 'everyday' drugs and medicines by the fact that they are illegal substances used for recreational purposes.

It is of course important to distinguish between different types of drugs because the norms that govern drug use vary with different types of drugs (Henderson, 1999) and the levels and frequency of use will be different depending on the types of drug we are talking about (Shiner and Newburn, 1997). Illicit drugs may be broadly grouped into the following six 'families':

- the cannabis family (marijuana, hash)
- the stimulant family (amphetamines, cocaine, crack)
- the opiate family (heroin, morphine, opium, methadone)
- the hallucinogenic family (LSD, magic mushrooms, peyote, phsilocibin)
- the volatile substance family (inhalants, glue, gas, amyl nitrate)
- the 'designer drug' family (most commonly ecstasy, although others are being invented and brought onto the market all the time)

These different 'families' of drugs are classified in law according to the ways in which their harmfulness is perceived. Different penalties are imposed (for possession and trafficking) depending on the classification of the drug. Maximum penalties are highest for class 'A' drugs, such as heroin, cocaine, ecstasy and LSD and lowest for class 'C' drugs such as tranquillisers and anabolic steroids (South, 1997). Cannabis and amphetamines are classified as Class 'B' drugs. A Police Foundation report has recently recommended that LSD, ecstasy and cannabis should be reclassified and that maximum penalties for possession of all drugs should be reduced. The government, however, appears to be unwilling to accept the recommendations of the report (Radio 4, 2000; Bennetto, 2000).

Each drug 'family' produces different effects in the user and may be used in different contexts and for different purposes (Measham *et al.*, 1998). On occasions, drugs from different 'families' may be combined. Indeed, evidence from various recent studies in this field suggests that there is a trend towards 'polyuse' amongst contemporary drug users (Hammersley *et al.*, 1999; Edmunds *et al.*, 1998; Parker *et al.*, 1998; South, 1997; Turnbull *et al.*, 1996; Tyler, 1995; Merchant and MacDonald; 1994). This means that contemporary drug users are likely to combine substances from different families, they may for example, take amphetamine or cocaine with cannabis or ecstasy.

In most cultures, across most of time, people have used drugs for their medicinal qualities, for recreation, or in religious ceremonies. In 2000 BC, for example, the Chinese used cannabis for making tea; in 1000 BC coca leaves were so highly valued amongst the Incas that they were used instead of silver and gold to barter for food and clothing; they were also chewed as an aid to digestion and used as an appetite suppressant. The Aztec Indians believed that eating peyote cactus and magic mushrooms brought them closer to God and these substances were widely used in religious ceremonies around 100 BC (Robson, 1999).

Most drugs that are classified as illicit in contemporary British society began their lives as legally available substances that were used for a variety of purposes. Below we briefly examine the history of a range of currently popular drugs in Britain, including alcohol and tobacco.

Alcohol

The origins of alcohol use are unclear but it appears to date back many thousands of years. Records show that wine was produced in Egypt as early as 3500 BC (Tyler, 1995: p. 52). In Britain, ale was 'the endemic tipple of the native population since pre-Roman times' and taverns began to appear around the twelfth century (Robson, 1999: p. 36). In Medieval Britain ale was safer to drink than water and was an important source of nutrition; it was routinely given to children who were encouraged to drink two or three glasses with a meal. In 1689, beer consumption in Britain was at an all time high with an average of 832 pints per year consumed for each man, woman and child. This had fallen to 200 pints, on average, by 1976 (Robson, 1999).

The seventeenth century view of alcohol as a benign drug, which was recommended by doctors for depression, venereal disease and gout, gave way in the eighteenth century to a view that alcohol was a social menace and that drunkenness was a 'disease'. From 1720–1750 the 'gin epidemic' exploded in Britain and during this period 8,000 'dram shops' opened in London where one could be 'drunk for a penny, dead drunk for tuppence' (Robson, 1999: p. 38). So great was official concern about drunkenness, that heavy taxes and curbs on retail sales were introduced at this time (Tyler, 1995).

Alcohol was considered the major substance abuse problem in Britain in the nineteenth century (Advisory Council on the Misuse of Drugs (ACMD), 1998) and in 1849 the term 'alcoholism' was first coined (Robson, 1999). Alcohol increasingly became a subject of public and official concern; temperance movements developed and the first licensing restrictions were imposed on public houses (Tyler, 1995).

During the First World War, respectable upper working class and lower middle class women began to frequent pubs in unprecedented numbers (Gutzke, 1994). It was at this time that the modern licensing system was introduced under the Defence of the Realm Act (DORA). The provisions of this Act were enacted in Civil Law in 1921 by the Licensing Act, which gave licensing powers to local magistrates (Tyler, 1995; South, 1997). In 1908, it became illegal for children under the age of fourteen to enter bars and, in 1923, the sale of alcohol to those under 18 was forbidden (Robson, 1999).

In the thirty year period from 1961–91 alcohol consumption in Britain rose by almost a third. Wines, spirits and cider all saw 'healthy gains' although there was a decline in sales of beer (Tyler, 1995). Currently, 93 per cent of British men and 87 per cent of British women consume some alcohol and in 1996, more than a quarter of all men and 14 per cent of women in Britain were drinking above the recommended safety levels (Robson, 1999). In contemporary Britain, alcohol consumption is twice as high as it was in the 1950s but remains much reduced when compared with levels of consumption in the eighteenth and nineteenth centuries (South, 1997). The 1990s saw the introduction of 'alcopops' or 'designer drinks', for example 'hooch', 'moonshine', 'Bacardi breezers', 'WKD', 'Moscow Mule', 'Red Square' and others. These products usually contain high volumes of alcohol relative to other alcoholic products and it has been suggested that they were cynically marketed and intended to capture the teenage market (Tyler, 1995; Robson, 1999; South, 1997). A recent study from the west of Scotland found that these drinks 'are a cause for concern' because they tend to be particularly attractive to 14–16-year-olds and appeal to them more than conventional drinks. The consumption of these drinks is also associated with 'drinking in less controlled environments, heavier drinking, and greater drunkenness' (Hughes *et al.*, 1997).

Alcohol is thought to be implicated in between 30,000 to 40,000 deaths each year in Britain and this country currently tops the league table for young people under the age of 17 experiencing alcohol-related problems (Alcohol Concern, 1991: pp. 4–6, cited in South, 1997: p. 927; Robson, 1999). Despite this, alcohol is widely advertised and available. It tends to be represented as a 'happy social lubricant' rather than as a 'hard drug' (Tyler, 1995). Certainly, the young people we spoke to were familiar with many of the designer drinks named above. Although they often recognised that alcohol was a drug, they did not appear to think of alcohol in the same way as they thought of other substances. Neither did they think of their alcohol consumption in terms of standard 'units'.

Tobacco

There is also some uncertainty as to the origins of the habit of smoking tobacco. It has been suggested that tobacco originated in Africa and was used in various parts of the world before being introduced to Europe (Matthee, 1998). Some evidence suggests that it may have been smoked in India around 2000 BC and it is known that it was smoked by Mayan Indians in Mexico around 500 AD (Tyler, 1995). Commercial trading in tobacco appears to have begun about 500 years ago and it was first introduced to Britain in 1565. For the first twenty years, its use was strictly medicinal. It was claimed that, amongst other things, tobacco could cure breast cancer and broken limbs. Boys at Eton were required to smoke a pipeful every morning or risk being flogged if they refused (Tyler, 1995). Sir Walter Raleigh is credited with introducing the 'fashionable London set' to tobacco in the late sixteenth century. It became increasingly popular in the seventeenth century amongst the wealthy and demand always outstripped supply (Robson, 1999). With the introduction of wood and clay pipes, tobacco smoking became more accessible to those who were not wealthy. King James I condemned the habit of smoking tobacco and, in 1604, published his *Counterblaste to Tobacco* in which he declared smoking was 'loathsome to the eye, hateful to the nose, harmful to the brain and dangerous to the lungs' (Robson, 1999: p. 55, q.v. Matthee, 1998: p. 33; Tyler, 1995; Ettorre, 1992). Moral objections to the habit, however, were soon overcome by economic considerations. King James introduced an import tax on tobacco and later established a royal import monopoly (Tyler, 1994; Matthee, 1998; Robson, 1999). By the end of the seventeenth century, sniffing snuff had become more popular than smoking tobacco and remained so until the nineteenth century (Tyler, 1995).

Cigarette making factories were introduced in the nineteenth century, the first factory in Britain being established in London in 1856. Automatic cigarette rolling machines were developed in 1881 (Tyler, 1995). At this time smoking was considered to be 'undermining the relationship between the sexes' (Lander, 1885, cited in Ettorre, 1992: p. 97). The demand for cigarettes increased rapidly towards the end of the century and by the end of the First World War, cigarettes had become the most popular method of consuming tobacco (Robson, 1999). In 1905, 11,000 million cigarettes were sold annually in the United Kingdom, by 1934 this had risen to 74,000 million. Prior to World War II, smoking was considered something 'nice girls don't do' (Montross, and Montross, 1923, cited in Ettorre, 1992: p. 94) and the majority of smokers were men. However, smoking became popular with women during the war and cigarette sales continued to rise (Robson, 1999). In America during World War II, President Roosevelt made tobacco a protected crop as part of the war effort (Taylor, 1984).

Consumption continued to increase after the war and, in Britain, 113,000 million cigarettes were being sold annually at this time. Sales peaked at 137,000 million in 1973 and have tended to decline slightly since then (Robson, 1999; Taylor, 1984). In 1961, 60 per cent of men and 50 per cent of women were smokers. In the 1950s and 1960s, smoking was most prevalent amongst higher income groups but by 1987 this pattern had reversed and 13 per cent of Social Class 1 were smokers compared to 46 per cent of Social Class 5 (Robson, 1999). As the Advisory Council on Drug Misuse reports, class differentials in smoking behaviour suggest that 'cigarettes in Britain are moving towards becoming a poverty drug' (ACMD, 1998: p. 103).

The health risks associated with smoking were identified, in both Britain and America, in the early 1960s and, as a result, television advertising of tobacco was banned in the United Kingdom in 1965. It was not until 1971, however, that health warnings on cigarette packets were introduced (Taylor, 1984). During the 1980s and 1990s, there has been a shift in public attitudes to smoking and in the General Household Survey (1996) 29 per cent of men and 28 per cent of women described themselves as 'regular smokers' (cited in Robson, 1999). Most new recruits to cigarette smoking are under 18 years of age and in 1994, 22 per cent of boys and 27 per cent of girls aged 15 were classified as regular smokers (ACMD, 1998: p. 70). The reduction in smoking since the 1970s has been more rapid amongst men than amongst women (Robson, 1999).

Smoking cigarettes and tobacco is thought to be responsible for 110,000 deaths in Britain each year (South, 1997; Robson, 1999). The health costs, however, are balanced against the revenue the government derives from taxes on cigarettes and tobacco. In 1979, for example, the British government provided more finance to the tobacco industry to modernise its plant and equipment than it did to the Health Education Authority to promote anti-smoking health campaigns (Taylor, 1984: p. 311). The majority of young people to whom we spoke smoked cigarettes and, as with alcohol, did not appear to think of cigarettes as a 'drug' in the same way as they thought of other substances. However, many did appear to be aware of the health risks associated with smoking cigarettes.

Cannabis

There is clear evidence that the Chinese were cultivating cannabis in the fourth century BC. In Britain, it was the Romans who first began cultivating it for rope making and weaving (Robson, 1999: p. 67). In the eighteenth century, cannabis began to be used in Britain as a herbal remedy for numerous ailments including labour pains and toothache. In the nineteenth century, although its recreational use was not widespread, it was available over the counter at chemists in England and Scotland (Robson, 1999). Queen Victoria is reputed to have used it to relieve menstrual cramps (Tyler, 1995). In 1925, the government ratified the Geneva Convention on 'the manufacture, sale and movement of dangerous drugs' (Robson, 1999: p. 69) and, as a result, cannabis was outlawed in Britain in 1928. The drug remained available, however, for use in psychiatry until it was 'absolutely prohibited' by the Misuse of Drugs Act 1971 (Robson, 1999)

There is some evidence of cannabis use amongst bohemians and jazz musicians in Britain in the 1950s (South, 1997) but it was not until the 1960s that the use of this substance 'exploded'. By 1970, 4 million people in Britain had tried it, including a third of all university students (Robson, 1999). Government alarm at this trend led to the commissioning of the Wootton Report (1968) which concluded that there were 'no harmful effects' associated with long-term, moderate use of the drug. The report recommended liberalisation of the law in relation to cannabis but its recommendations were 'dismissively rejected' (South, 1997: p. 940) and ignored by the Callaghan government (Robson, 1999).

Of the illicit drugs being considered here, cannabis is thought to have been 'most used ever' and in 1996, 27 per cent of men and 18 per cent of women between 16–59 years claimed to have used it (ACMD, 1998). In 1991, the cannabis trade within the European Union was estimated to be worth $7.5 billion per year, representing three times the size of the heroin market and worth $1 billion more than cocaine (Tyler, 1995). In the 1980s the police themselves began to call for changes in the law relating to cannabis and by the 1990s there had been an informal slackening of the law, whereby cautions were issued to first time offenders who were in possession of small amounts (Tyler, 1995: p. 178; South, 1997). More recently, the New Labour government has sanctioned the use of cannabis for medical research purposes and its anti-drug strategy has acknowledged a need to concentrate on those drugs 'that do the most damage' such as heroin and cocaine (President of the Council, 1998; Rayner, 2000). Recently, the Police Foundation has recommended that cannabis be reclassified and that possession should no longer be an imprisonable offence. The government, however, appears reluctant to change the law. Amongst the young people to whom we spoke, cannabis was the most widely and most frequently used illicit substance.

Opiates and cocaine

In nineteenth century Britain, the medicinal use of opiates and cocaine was largely unregulated (Pearson, 1999; Robson, 1999). Opium was regularly used as a medicine 'by most ordinary Englishmen' (sic) (Parssinen, 1983: p. 51) and opiate use was widely accepted across all classes. Opium was recommended even for those who were healthy because it was considered to 'optimise the internal equilibrium of the human body' (Robson, 1999: p. 172). The history of opium in Britain is of course tied up with British political and economic history of the eighteenth and nineteenth centuries. The conquest of Bengal in 1773 gave Britain a monopoly of Indian opium after which the East India Company set about exporting large amounts to China. China's attempts to resist these imports led to what have become known as the 'Opium Wars' of 1839–1842 and 1856–60 (ibid). As South (1997: p. 935) has argued, British economic interests in opium make it hardly surprising that domestic use was largely unregulated in the nineteenth century.

The recreational use of opium was associated with mill towns such as those found in Nottinghamshire and Lancashire, where, in 1801, a local chemist estimated that 'women users outnumbered men by three to one' (Parssinen, 1983: p. 47). Evidence from the United States has also suggested that in the nineteenth century, two thirds of those addicted to opiates were women (Courtwright, 1992, cited in Pearson, 1999: p. 477). In the fenlands of Norfolk, Cambridgeshire and Lincolnshire, the practice of eating opium was so widespread that this area was known to the Victorians as 'the opium district' (Parssinen, 1983: p. 49, q.v. Tyler, 1995; South, 1997; Robson, 1999). Although eating opium was common in the nineteenth century, the practice of smoking it was regarded as 'a rather vile alien indulgence' (Robson, 1999: p. 172) that was associated with Chinese seamen and confined to the area of Limehouse in London (Parssinen, 1983, Tyler, 1995, South, 1997). In 1909, as a result of concerns about both immigration and the practice of smoking opium, the London County Council introduced a by-law to prohibit the smoking of opium in 'licensed seamen's boarding houses' (Parssinen, 1983).

Perhaps the most disreputable use of opium in the nineteenth century was as a baby 'calmer' (Parssinen, 1983; South, 1997, Robson, 1999). The practice of feeding children opium, in the form of laudanum, or 'Godfrey's Cordial', was widespread across classes and popularly accepted in different geographical regions. It was most commonly associated with areas where 'women worked in factories, in cottage industries, or in agricultural gangs' (Parssinen, 1983: p. 42). Many children died each year from opium poisoning but adults were rarely charged with causing the death of a child in this way. When they were so charged, juries were reluctant to convict them, especially if they were related to the child (Parssinen, 1983: p. 44).

Morphine was first isolated from opium in 1805 by a German chemist and, by 1825, it was being marketed as a cure for opium addiction. Heroin was not isolated until 1874, and it too was marketed as a 'safe, non-addictive substitute for morphine'. Commercial production of heroin began in 1898 (Tyler, 1995: p. 306).

The practice of chewing coca leaves was widespread in the ancient civilisations of South America but it was not until the 1850s that the alkaloid 'cocaine' was first isolated from the plant and the qualities of the drug became widely publicised (Parssinen, 1983; Kohn, 1999; Robson, 1999). In the 1880s, Sigmund Freud wrote 'a song of praise to this magical substance' after it had apparently cured his friend, who became the first known cocaine addict, of his morphine addiction (Robson, 1999: p. 88; Tyler, 1995: p. 198). In 1886 the drink *Coca-Cola* was introduced and marketed as a 'refreshing and stimulating alternative to alcohol'. Each glass contained a few milligrams of cocaine until 1903, when the cocaine was replaced by caffeine (Robson, 1999: p. 88).

Towards the end of the nineteenth century, the sale of cocaine and opium were restricted to registered pharmacists by the Poisons and Pharmacy Act of 1868 (Robson, 1999; South, 1997; Parssinen, 1983). This resulted from pressure exerted by pharmacists who were anxious to establish a monopoly over the supply of drugs (Holloway, 1998) in addition to growing concerns about the addictive properties of cocaine, and the numbers of people dying annually from opium poisoning.

In the nineteenth century, there had been a rather 'laissez-faire' approach to drugs on the part of British governments, but anxieties about drug use emerged in the early twentieth century and the government approach changed (Parssinen, 1983; South, 1997; Pearson, 1999; Robson, 1999; Kohn, 1999). At this time cocaine was the most popular 'street drug' (Parssinen, 1983; Kohn, 1999; Robson, 1999) and it 'dominated the first underground British drug scene' (Kohn, 1999: p. 105) which was confined to approximately one square mile in London's West End (Kohn, 1999; Parssinen, 1983). Cocaine was sold in the streets of Soho and in pubs on Charing Cross Road and Shaftsbury Avenue (Parssinen, 1983). The use of cocaine was particularly associated with women; 'prostitutes, actresses and dancers', rather than with any particular 'sub-culture' (Kohn, 1999; Parssinen, 1983).

Concern about drug use first emerged during the First World War. In the period 1910–1930 'the public was deluged with a mass of fact and opinion about drugs' (Parssinen, 1983: p. 115). Kohn (1999: p. 105) has argued that in a six-month period at the end of 1915, 'cocaine turned from miracle to menace'. The status of cocaine was transformed because it was thought to pose a threat to soldiers (Parssinen, 1983; Kohn, 1999; Robson, 1999). Soldiers on leave in London 'were keen to get hold of anything that might make life in the trenches more bearable' (Robson, 1999) and could buy morphine and cocaine kits at Harrods. These contained a syringe and spare needles and were labelled, 'A Useful Present for Friends at the Front' (Robson, 1999: p. 175). *The Times* in this period reported that drugs posed a threat to soldiers that was 'more deadly than bullets' (Kohn, 1999: p. 113).

As a result of these concerns, regulation 40B of the Defence of the Realm Act (DORA) was introduced in June 1916 and opium and cocaine became regulated as narcotic drugs rather than as poisons (Parssinen, 1983; Tyler, 1995; South, 1997; Kohn, 1999). The DORA regulations targeted cocaine but opium was also restricted and it became illegal to supply 'intoxicants' to members of the armed forces (Parssinen, 1983: p. 131). DORA regulation 40B (with many extra restrictions) was enacted in Civil Law in 1920 as the first Dangerous Drugs Act (Robson, 1999; Kohn, 1999). This made possession of morphine, heroin, opium or cocaine illegal without a prescription.

From the 1920s through to the 1960s, doctors were able to prescribe morphine, heroin and cocaine. At this time, opioid addicts were few in number and, for the most part, geographically and socially confined to the 'professional classes' in London. Few 'working class' addicts were known to doctors at this time and the opioid situation remained fairly stable (Robson, 1999: p. 176). Alarmed by the falling age of addicts in 1960s America, however, the Government decided to review the situation in Britain. The first Brain Committee Report (1961) reported that 'nothing much had changed' since the 1920s. It soon became evident, however, that the 'drug scene' was changing and the Brain Committee was reconvened in 1964 (Robson, 1999; South, 1997; Tyler, 1995). In 1960, 454 addicts were known to the Home Office and by 1964, this number had increased to 753 (South, 1997). It was thought that these 'new addicts' in the 1960s were the consequence of 'leakage' of narcotics into the illicit market as a result of over-prescribing by doctors (South, 1997; Tyler, 1995). There was 'virtually no criminally organised black market in Britain at the time' (Robson, 1999: p. 178) and seizures by the police were mainly of pharmaceutical (rather than imported) heroin. The second report from the Brain committee therefore acknowledged that drug addiction was a growing problem that required 'drastic practical measures' (ibid).

The second Brain report resulted in the establishment of Drug Dependency Units (DDUs) and the imposition of restrictions on who could prescribe heroin and cocaine. The right to prescribe was limited to psychiatrists working in the DDUs who were compulsorily obliged to notify the Home Office of drug addicts, thus the confidentiality of the doctor patient relationship was undermined. In addition, the Misuse of Drugs Act (1971) was passed. In 1967, there were 2,000 known heroin addicts in Britain (Robson, 1999: p. 178), mainly confined to London and the south-east 'with a handful of users in other major cities' (Stimson, 1987: p. 39). Heroin addiction continued to grow, however, despite the new restrictions and in the four-year period from 1973–77, the Home Office was notified of 4,607 new addicts.

It was in the 1980s, however, that the drug problem in Britain entirely changed (Pearson, 1999). At this time an 'epidemic' of heroin use developed (Pearson, 1999; Parker *et al.*, 1998; Collison, 1996; Dorn and South, 1987) and it is argued that the heroin problem has now become 'endemic' (Parker *et al.*, 1998). It was in this period that drugs such as heroin 'migrated from Piccadilly Circus and the Fulham Road' (Pitts, 2001 forthcoming) to become a working class youth phenomenon across the rest of the country. Thus, in the four-year period from 1981–85, the Home Office was notified of 21,030 new addicts (South, 1997). Many of these new addicts were under twenty-five (British Youth Council, 1992).

Heroin use has spread geographically and socially: it appears to recognise no national or class boundaries, and the age of those using it has become younger. In 1990, approximately a third of all Home Office notified addicts were under 25 and in that year 45 per cent of newly notified addicts were under this age (British Youth Council, 1992). A recent report has shown that the average age at which young people begin to use heroin has fallen markedly to *fifteen*. This is two years younger than average age of first use in the mid-1980s (Eggington and Parker, cited in Travis, 2000). *The Guardian* has recently reported that a twelve-year-old has been convicted of dealing in heroin and crack-cocaine. By 1996, the Home Office had been notified of 43,372 addicts (ACMD, 1998).

Most of the cases notified to the Home Office are addicted to heroin, methadone or cocaine. Of course, not all of those who are addicted are in touch with drug services and not all of those who are addicted are notified to the Home Office (ACMD, 1998: p. 9). These figures therefore represent an under-estimation of the scale of the actual problem. A recent study, for example, has suggested that there are between 130,000 and 200,000 problem drug users in England (Edmunds *et al.*, 1998). Since 1987 there has been a fivefold increase in drug use amongst 12–13-year-olds and an eightfold increase amongst 14–15-year-olds. The UK currently has 'more 15 and 16-year-old drug users than any other EU country' (National Strategy for Neighbourhood Renewal, 2000).

The spread of heroin use combined with concerns about AIDS and HIV infection drove public policy, in the 1980s and early 1990s, in the direction of harm minimisation (South, 1999). In this period, needle exchange schemes were established and the practice of prescribing methadone as a substitute for heroin became widespread (Robson, 1999; Tyler, 1995). In the 1990s, with evidence of the link between drugs and crime, the policy agenda shifted from public health concerns to concerns about criminal justice and 'community safety' (Pearson, 1999; Parker *et al.*, 1998). It is these latter concerns that have driven much of drug policy in the 1990s (Barton, 1999).

If, in the early 1980s we were concerned about the spread of heroin use, later in the 1980s, official alarm about cocaine use re-emerged as a result of the 'epidemic' of crack-cocaine in the USA (South, 1997; Tyler, 1995). In the 1960s, cocaine use had not been popular with the youth culture of the day because it was associated with heroin-injecting 'junkies' (Tyler, 1995). In the 1970s, it re-entered the drug scene as a drug that could be sniffed rather than injected and in the 1980s, the smokeable form of 'crack' appeared. Murji (1999: p. 55) has argued that since the late 1980s, 'cocaine has been the drug most linked with 'race' in Britain'. He shows that journalism has made explicit the association between black people, 'Yardies' and 'crack' (see for example, Davison, 1997). Tyler (1995) has observed that crack use in Britain was originally confined to black communities but by the 1990s had spread to white drug-using areas as well. It has often wreaked havoc in those communities (see for example, Pettiway, 1997; Bourgois, 1996). A recent report found that three-quarters of the 15–20-year-olds interviewed had tried crack-cocaine and one third had used it in the month before the interview (Eggington and Parker cited in Travis, 2000). Similarly, a relatively high proportion of the young people in this study had used drugs such as heroin, crack or cocaine. Given their highly addictive properties, this indeed suggests a worrying trend.

Amphetamines

Amphetamine ('speed') was first synthesised towards the end of the nineteenth century (1887) and was used for a number of medical conditions from the 1930s. Amphetamine was first marketed in 1932 as a nasal decongestant and soon after was used in the treatment of asthma, obesity and depression (Robson, 1999; Tyler, 1995).

The first non-medical use of amphetamine in Britain was by soldiers in the Second World War to counter fatigue. Hitler also received regular daily injections of the drug (Robson, 1999; Tyler, 1995). Many amphetamine based products were available over the counter in the 1950s and during the Suez Crisis of 1956, Prime Minister Anthony Eden declared that he was 'living on benzedrine' (Tyler, 1995: p. 82). Amphetamine was not regulated in Britain until 1956 and after this time, it was available on prescription only. Unlike heroin and cocaine, however, any doctor could prescribe it. In 1964, nearly four million prescriptions were issued (Robson, 1999; Tyler, 1995).

Amphetamine became popular in the underground drug scene of the 1960s (South, 1997). The use of 'Purple Hearts' (drinamyl), a mixture of amphetamine and barbiturate, was especially popular with the 'mods' of that era and they were used regularly by 'thousands' of 'ordinary' youth (Robson, 1999; Tyler, 1995). 'Purple hearts' were replaced in the 1970s by 'black bombers' (durophet-m) but both have since been withdrawn from the market. In 1964, the Drugs (Prevention of Misuse) Act tightened the law in relation to amphetamine, and made unlicensed possession and importation an offence (Tyler, 1995). The illicit market, however, continued to expand (Robson, 1999; Tyler, 1995) and 1967–68 was regarded as an 'epidemic year' (Tyler, 1995). As a result of government pressure the number of prescriptions for amphetamine fell from the mid-1960s into the 1970s but this merely encouraged the development of illicit production by local manufacturers (Robson, 1999; Tyler, 1995).

By the early 1990s, amphetamine had firmly established itself in the new dance scene throughout the United Kingdom (Tyler, 1995) and after cannabis, it is now the most widely used illicit drug amongst young people (Robson, 1999; ACMD, 1998; Parker *et al.*, 1998; South, 1997; Tyler, 1995). In some parts of the country, notably Essex, young people have moved from sniffing to injecting amphetamine and have begun to use heroin to 'take the edge off' the 'speed' (Tyler, 1995: p. 93). Next to cannabis, amphetamine was the drug most used by the young people in this study. It seemed often to be used interchangeably with other drugs such as ecstasy or cocaine.

LSD and hallucinogenics

Hallucinogenic plants were used thousands of years ago in ancient civilisations for religious festivals and ceremonies (Robson, 1999). In the form of LSD, however, hallucinogenics are a relatively modern addition to the array of drugs available in Europe. Lysergic acid diethylamide-25 (LSD) was first discovered accidentally by the scientist Albert Hoffman in 1943. He had isolated this chemical five years previously when searching for a new heart stimulant. In 1943, he came to realise its potential in psychiatric applications after he accidentally ingested some. LSD was first marketed in 1949 and its medical and psychiatric use expanded rapidly. In the 1950s, it is estimated that over 100,000 patients were receiving it in America and Europe (Robson, 1999).

The hippie 'Cultural Revolution' of the 1960s saw the consumption of LSD rise phenomenally. In America, for example, 25,000 people had used LSD recreationally in 1962 and this figure had risen to 4 million by 1965. Its virtues were extolled by some high profile academics, amongst them Dr. Timothy Leary (Tyler, 1995) and Michael Foucault (Macey, 1993). In Britain, in 1966, production of LSD for the licit market stopped after the drug had been proscribed in the same year and, after 1967, media 'scare stories' multiplied (Tyler, 1995). Law enforcement became more resolute and underground chemists were apprehended and convicted. For a period between the mid-1970s and the 1980s LSD was in short supply, but with the advent of Acid House music and the dance, drug, and club culture the illicit trade recovered. LSD made a comeback and has been widely available in Britain and the USA (Robson, 1999; South, 1997; Tyler, 1995). Many of the young people discussed here had used LSD.

Ecstasy and 'dance' drugs

These 'designer' drugs are the most recent to appear in the illicit drugs market, so called because existing drugs are re-synthesised and their chemical-molecular structure altered. In 1910, a German chemist synthesised the parent drug of ecstasy (MDA) (Tyler, 1995). Methylenedioxymethamphetamine (MDMA, ecstasy) was formulated in 1912 and patented in 1914. It was legally available 'from around 1970' but was outlawed in 1976 in Britain by an amendment to the Misuse of Drugs Act which proscribed all 'amphetamine-like compounds' (Robson, 1999: p. 138). At the same time favourable reports about the drug's benefits in psychiatric settings were appearing. As with LSD, the market for ecstasy in Britain rapidly expanded with the advent of the rave culture and modern club scene (Robson, 1999: p. 139; Tyler, 1995; Merchant and MacDonald, 1994). Estimates of prevalence vary but most commentators agree that ecstasy and its derivatives 'have been a familiar commodity to many hundreds of thousands of young people over the last decade' (Robson, 1999: p. 139; Parker *et al.*, 1998; Measham *et al.*, 1998; Merchant and MacDonald, 1994). It is thought that half a million young people take the drug every week. In 1993, the 'rave' business was estimated to be worth £2 billion per annum, 'with a million youngsters spending £35 million every week' (Tyler, 1995: p. 251). Certainly many of the young people we spoke to had used ecstasy. This was one of a range of substances available in their 'pharmacological filofax' (Collison, 1996).

Volatile substances

The origins of sniffing mind-altering substances can be traced to ancient civilisations but the modern practice of sniffing for recreational pleasure is rooted in the nineteenth century when substances such as nitrous oxide, ether and chloroform were fashionable and widely available (Tyler, 1995: p. 357; Robson, 1999: p. 127). In the 1950s, poor American youth who were unable to afford alcohol or other intoxicants took to the practice of sniffing solvents. This brought the recreational use of solvents to the attention of a wider public although British public interest in this form of substance use was not aroused until the 1970s when glue sniffing was being reported throughout the British Isles (Robson, 1999). Glue sniffing provided the majority of newspaper 'scare' stories until the arrival of the heroin 'epidemic' in the 1980s.

By the 1980s, use of volatile substances had become attractive to young people, particularly those in the North of England and Scotland (Robson, 1999; Tyler, 1995) and was especially associated with punks and skinheads (Tyler, 1995). Solvent use has traditionally been associated with poor, working class, inner city youth (ACMD, 1998) and between 1981 and 1990 solvents killed four times as many people from the lowest social class as from the highest social class (Tyler, 1995: p. 358). Eighty per cent of deaths from solvents are amongst young people and most of them are under 17 (Robson, 1999: p. 130). In 1991, 38 per cent of those who died from solvent use had used them for the first time (Tyler, 1995). More boys tend to die than girls, although there is some conflicting evidence about whether boys use them more (see Robson, 1999; Tyler, 1999; Henderson, 1999).

In 1985, the Intoxicating Substances Act was passed in Britain which made it an offence to supply anyone under 18 with a substance which they knew, or had reason to believe, would be used 'to achieve intoxication' (Robson, 1999: p. 130). This was accompanied by a major public health campaign. Perhaps as a result of these measures, mortality rates for death by volatile substances have declined over the past ten years (Robson, 1999). The use of volatile substances was fairly widespread amongst the young people considered here and certainly more widespread than studies of young people in the general population have suggested.

Young People, Drugs and Moral Panics

Drug use in British society has, since the beginning of the twentieth century, provided a source for sensationalist media coverage, often playing on fears about inter-racial mixing (Tyler, 1995; Ruggerio and South, 1997; Murji, 1999; Kohn, 1999). In turn such reporting has triggered various 'moral panics' (Cohen 1973) amongst the authorities (Parssinen, 1983; Kohn, 1999). A 'moral panic' occurs when 'a condition, episode, person or group of persons emerges to become defined as a threat to societal values and interests' (Cohen 1973, cited in Dutton, 1986).

In relation to drugs, such panics initially focused on 'the degenerate Chinaman living in East London's dock area and peddling drugs and vice to tender white young things' (Tyler, 1995: p. 203). In the 1920s, journalists wrote about 'dance-dope dens' in London, 'where "the same sickening crowd of undersized aliens" mingled with "pretty, underdressed" young English girls' (Parssinen, 1983: p. 168). The focus of these panics was inter-racial mixing and the use of cocaine and opium. Similar panics followed in the 1950s in relation to cannabis use (Tyler, 1995). In the *Sunday Graphic* a journalist reported that, 'Hemp, marijuana and hashish represent a thoroughly unsavoury trade' and that the (predominately black) men involved in it were 'the most evil men who have ever taken to the vice business' (Tyler, 1995: pp. 169–170). Again there were racist tones to this reporting and concerns about 'foreigners' corrupting 'young white girls' (Murji, 1999; Kohn, 1999; Tyler, 1995).

Sensationalist media coverage followed for LSD in the 1970s, solvents in the 1980s and ecstasy, crack, heroin and drugs in general in the 1990s (*The Independent on Sunday*, 1990, 1992; *The Independent*, 1993, 1994; *The Guardian*, 1994). *Time Out*, for example, recently issued a drugs 'special issue' with the headline 'One in three Londoners go to work on drugs' (Bloomfield and Kerr, 2000) and *The Guardian* recently had as its front page headline, 'Heroin: abusers start at 15' (Travis, 2000).

In addition to the panics that have been elaborated around drugs by the British media, public, popular and political discourse has often cast different elements of youth culture as modern day 'folk devils' around whom 'moral panics' have coalesced (Cohen, 1973; Merchant and MacDonald, 1994; Shapiro, 1999). In the 1980s, by demonising young people in general, and those who were unemployed in particular, Margaret Thatcher's government was provided with a convenient formula for holding the casualties of social and economic transformations responsible for their own condition (Craine, 1997). Parker and colleagues (1998: p. 4) argue that by the early 1990s the media had established a chain of equivalence between 'drugs-crime-danger-youth' that was translated into public policy. 'Blaming youth' and 'reducing complex social issues to soundbites' had become a 'device of government' (Parker *et al.*, 1998). Thus, by the 1990s, homeless young people and people engaged in begging had become the subjects of moral panics in their own right (Jordan, 1999; Dean and Gale, 1999; Jones, 1997; Blackman, 1997).

In the early 1990s, with the advent of 'raves' and 'rave culture', young people and their use of recreational drugs became the subject of another panic that served to fuel public anxieties around the issue of drugs and young people. The media promoted 'ravers as the new 'folk devils' and in 1990, 'draconian measures' were introduced to 'quash' the 'rave culture' under The Entertainments (Increased Penalties) Act (Merchant and MacDonald, 1994). In 1993, new powers to 'crack down' on 'ravers' were announced by the then Home Secretary (Merchant and MacDonald, 1994: p. 17) and in The Criminal Justice Act 1994 the police were given more powers to prevent 'raves' from taking place. Since March, 1997, as the result of a government-backed private members bill, local councils have had powers to close clubs at once where they find evidence of drug use or drug dealing (Shapiro, 1999: p. 31).

In 1994 the Conservative government responded to the increased use of drugs by young people by launching its *Tackling Drugs Together* initiative. This rested on three main assumptions: firstly, that young people were vulnerable to drug misuse as a result of succumbing to peer pressure, secondly, that drugs are both a danger and a menace, and thirdly, that drug users pose a threat to local communities because of the crime in which they engage to fund their drug taking activities. The New Labour government continued the offensive against drugs with its new ten-year anti-drugs strategy (President of the Council, 1998).

Contemporary Fears

Contemporary attitudes to drugs have been shaped by discourses which have tended to cast the use of illicit drugs as aberrant or strange while the use of legal intoxicants such as alcohol, tobacco, tea and coffee have been viewed as 'normal'. They have thus served to define those who use illicit drugs as 'outsiders' from mainstream culture (South, 1999; Becker, 1963). As the historical evidence presented above demonstrates, however, this is a phenomenon peculiar to the twentieth century in western societies (South, 1999; Collison, 1996) and many 'public anxieties' now cluster around the issue of drugs (Pearson, 1999).

A study by the Forensic Science Services that carried out drug tests on a million employees in 1998, found that drug consumption was widespread across all age groups. The study concluded that 'drug abuse is so prevalent amongst British workers that one in ten, including the over 60s and senior executives are testing positive for illicit substances' (Carter, 1998). A recent survey of *Time Out* readers concluded that 89 per cent of the total sample admitted to being 'regular' drug users (Bloomfield and Kerr, 2000). Much of the available evidence therefore appears to support the idea that drug use has become 'normalised' in the culture of contemporary Britain (Pearson, 1999; South, 1999; Parker *et al*., 1998; Merchant and MacDonald, 1994). This thesis suggests that drug use, especially cannabis, is socially acceptable amongst many groups, and particularly amongst the young, whether they use drugs themselves or not (Pearson, 1999).

On the other hand, Shiner and Newburn (1997, 1999) reject the idea of 'normalisation' by pointing out that young people often hold restrictive views about drugs, and, although a large proportion have taken drugs, an even larger proportion have not. However, as South (1999: p. 4) argues, 'the sheer scale of social activity around drug use in contemporary society does suggest that it is now actually a part of the "paramount reality" of everyday life'. That is, in Western culture, 'personal and popular awareness of drugs as a social, lifestyle and crime related issue is now pretty universal' (South, 1999: p. 5, q.v. Pearson, 1999; Parker *et al*., 1998). For young people growing up in this 'chemical culture' (Henderson, 1999) 'whether or not they become drug users is a decision based on personal and peer group choice since the availability is a normal part of the leisure-pleasure landscape' (Parker *et al*., 1995).

All the drugs discussed in this chapter had been used by the young people who took part in this study. Drug taking was regarded more or less seriously by some, depending on the drugs we were talking about, for example, a sixteen-year-old young man said:

> *Personally, there's drugs that I won't touch like ecstasy, heroin, they're drugs I haven't touched. I've tried every other drug in the book an' that. I'm not really proud of it but I've tried it as a teenager like…I've seen people, as a child I was always scared of heroin because my dad knew someone that used to take heroin and he used to take it in front of little kids as well…still, I've got friends that ummm, smoke a bit of brown every now and then but I wouldn't touch it.*

On the other hand, cannabis was widely acknowledged to be 'harmless' and many thought it should be legalised:

> *I don't see a problem with smoking it [cannabis]. I believe, everyone says it's weird, but I believe that God put cannabis on this earth as a stimulant…If nobody made a problem out of it, no-one made a big hoo-ha, the government, and 'Oh don't smoke it, don't smoke it' then I think it would be just as common as coffee and how many people, like teenagers, drink coffee to how many teenagers smoke gear?*

Conclusion

In the eyes of these young people, alcohol and tobacco appeared to be more 'normalised' than other substances and, in particular, they appeared to underestimate the potential damage that alcohol may potentially inflict. What must concern us in the contemporary debate on drug use is the young ages at which the young people who took part in this study had started using drugs, especially cannabis, although it was also clear that other substances such as cocaine, amphetamine, ecstasy and even heroin appeared to be easily accessible to those who, legally, are not even old enough to drink. This must be a concern for all practitioners working with young people, in whatever capacity.

Later in this book, the discussion of drug use amongst the young people who took part in this study demonstrates the importance of recognising the link between drug use and other social problems. In the following chapter, however, we explore the question of whether there is something about the character of contemporary society that may make young people in general (Parker *et al.*, 1998), and vulnerable young people in particular, more prone to using drugs.

Chapter 2

Contemporary Society: Vulnerable and Disadvantaged Youth

Introduction

This chapter explores:

- what 'youth' means
- the historical and social context in which young people, especially vulnerable young people such as those who took part in the study, make the journey to adulthood
- the impact on young people, especially vulnerable young people of:
  - the major social policy developments of the 1980s and 1990s
  - the historical and cultural changes since the 1980s
- the extent to which these historical and cultural shifts account for increasing numbers of young people becoming involved in drug use.

What Do We Mean by 'Youth'?

'Youth' is the term used to refer to that period of life between 'childhood' and 'adulthood'. It is a culturally variable concept that is as much socially constructed as that of 'drugs'. It is also a concept that is specific to modern societies and does not denote some inevitable biological state. The boundaries between 'childhood', 'youth' and 'adulthood' are not clearly drawn or demarcated. The laws that define the rights and obligations of young people contribute to this ambiguity and young people often bear the legal responsibilities of citizenship without enjoying the political or social rights that accompany it (Dean, 1997). A young person, for example, may work and pay taxes, or be conscripted into the army at sixteen but cannot vote or stand for Parliament until they are eighteen. A young person is held to be criminally responsible at ten (eight in Scotland) and is therefore 'assumed to be morally competent' (Dean, 1997: p. 56) but a young woman may not consent to sex until she is sixteen, although she may be prescribed the contraceptive pill before this age. She may also be legally charged with soliciting to sell sex from the age of ten (Melrose *et al.*, 1999; Melrose and Brodie, 1999; Edwards, 1998). These and other anomalies mean that the period of adolescence may be a deeply confusing time for many young people and those concerned with their welfare.

The concept of 'youth' tends to impose a false homogeneity on a diverse group of people and set of social experiences. Working class and middle class youth, for example, may have increasingly polarised social experiences: exclusion from school or unemployment on the one hand versus university and rewarding careers on the other. Social class, gender, ethnicity and sexuality differentiate the experience of all young people although policy makers are not always sensitive to these differences. The government, for example, has announced its intention to 'break the link between drugs and crime' but has focused predominantly on acquisitive (and largely male) crime. This may reduce the number of burglaries and street crimes, and look good in performance targets, but it does little to respond to the needs of many young women who become involved in prostitution in order to finance their drug taking (May *et al.*, 2000; Melrose *et al.*, 1999; Crosby and Barrett, 1999; O'Neill *et al.*, 1995).

In relation to drugs in particular, there is evidence that ethnicity and gender are axes along which differences between young people emerge. Young white people are more likely than young people from ethnic minority groups to use drugs (Graham and Bowling, 1995; Ramsey, 1999). Although differences appear to be diminishing (McCallum, 1998; Parker *et al.*, 1998) drug use amongst young men, for example, is generally more prevalent than amongst young women (Graham and Bowling, 1995; Ramsay, 1999). This theme is picked up in Chapter 7 where gender differences in drug consumption patterns are explored. In the following section, some debates about the character of the contemporary social world and the position of young people within it are explored.

Young People and Contemporary Society

Inequality of wealth and income is now more deeply entrenched in Britain than it was twenty years ago (Scott, 1994; Hills, 1995; Barclay, 1995; Jordan, 1996; Dean with Melrose, 1998). So deeply entrenched, in fact, that Townsend (1996) has recently argued that inequality in Britain is as great as it is in Nigeria. The gap between the highest and lowest paid is as great as it was in 1886 (Glyn and Miliband cited in Tyler, 1995). This survey revealed that the top one per cent of income earners had received 93 times as much per head in tax cuts as the bottom 50 per cent in the period 1979–92. In the 30 year period from 1961–91 the income share of the richest tenth of the population increased from two per cent to 25 per cent while that of the poorest tenth fell from four point two per cent to three per cent (Barclay, 1995). The Conservative government's own figures revealed that the poorest tenth of the population experienced a 17 per cent fall in real income between 1979–92 while the richest tenth had experienced a 62 per cent increase (*The Guardian*, 1994 cited in Tyler, 1995). A survey by the Office of National Statistics (ONS) has recently shown that this trend has continued under the New Labour government (cited in Coyle and Grice, 2000).

There is a consensus in much of the literature that the contemporary social world we inhabit is centrally a world of consumption rather than production. It is also argued that self-identities are increasingly constructed through consumption (Collison, 1996: p. 430). This means that consuming particular types of commodities, (clothes, music, leisure activities and even drugs) enables particular identities to be constructed. These identities in turn signal that one 'belongs' (or does not belong) to particular social groups (Sidorenko-Stephenson, 1999), lifestyle sectors or 'imagined communities' (Anderson, 1991). It is useful to employ a 'double focus' when thinking about the activity of consumption (Morley, 1991) be it of drugs or any other commodity. It can then be understood as an activity that takes place in the realms of 'everyday life' *and* as a process that operates within the realm of ideology (Morley, 1991).

Of course, the prerequisite of a lifestyle based on, or constructed through, consumption is sufficient money to consume and our discussion of economic inequality in Britain suggests that this is not an activity equally available to all. Furthermore, the social structural changes that result from globalised markets have spawned 'serious economic exclusion amongst sections of the young population' (MacDonald, 1997b: p. 170) leaving many of them, such as those we spoke to in the course of this study, without the wherewithal to consume.

It is in this unequal and uncertain world that both 'mainstream' and 'excluded' youth, that is young people who have been cast to the margins of society as a result of economic, social and political change, such as those who took part in the study, make their journey to adulthood. For many of these their journeys are characterised by risk, insecurity and inequality. It has been suggested that because of the 'novelty' of their situation, young people represent something of a 'vanguard generation'. They are obliged to 'negotiate a new set of rules and expectations, new cultural pressures, new pathways to 'identity' and adulthood' (Parker *et al.*, 1998: p. 28).

The contemporary literature on 'youth' suggests that there are three key sites in which young people achieve the transition to adulthood:

1. in the transition from school to the labour market (from economic dependence to economic autonomy)

2. in establishing independent homes of their own and achieving domestic autonomy

3. in forming relationships: moving from the family of origin to the family of destination   (Coles, 1986).

A wealth of evidence however, suggests that in recent years increasing numbers of young people, like many of those who took part in this study, have become 'frozen in a state of perpetual youth or adolescence' (Pitts, 1999; Dean, 1997; France, 1996). They have been prevented from making the transition 'from adolescence to other higher status adult roles because they simply do not have the means to do so' (Pitts, 1999). Those young people who are socially and economically marginalised are, 'quite literally, prevented from growing up' (Pitts, 1999, q.v. Coles and Craig, 1999). It is these young people who are the 'casualties' of recent economic, political and social transformations (Burton *et al.*, 1989, q.v. Roche and Tucker, 1997; Kumar, 1993; Bradshaw, 1990) and who are now 'significantly structurally disadvantaged' as they attempt to make the transition to adulthood (Coles, 1995).

The developments that have resulted in this state of affairs are explored below. Here it is worth considering whether, in circumstances where young people's transition to adulthood is thwarted, they may be more likely to use symbolic means, such as smoking, drinking and consuming particular types of drugs, to signify their maturity and autonomy. In other words, by denying young people routes to autonomy, or by putting obstacles in the way of its attainment, do we make it more likely that some young people will take drugs?

The following section explores:

- the inter-related developments that have served to keep young people like those being discussed here 'young'
- whether this may incline them, more than teenagers of previous decades, to take drugs and to develop more problematic patterns of drug use.

Young People and the Labour Market

'Thatcherism', 'Reaganomics', and now the 'Third Way' represented by the New Labour government, have attempted to create labour markets that conform to the dictates of international economic forces (Whiteside, 1995: p. 69). In the process of transforming the labour market in line with the needs of the international economy, 'Thatcherism' heralded in an 'assault on youth' which functioned as a 'rhetorical smokescreen' to obscure the consequences of what, in 1983, Dennis Healey called 'Sado-Monetarism' (Craine, 1997: p. 131). Young people were demonised by neo-liberal discourses (Craine, 1997; Jones, 1997) and targeted by neo-liberal policies that attempted, wherever possible, to transfer responsibility for them from the state to the family (Bottomley, 1994 cited in Dean, 1997: p. 59).

National and international developments have ensured that, since the early 1980s, the youth labour market has virtually collapsed (Maguire and Maguire, 1997) and that unemployment has been a central feature in the lives of many young people (Craine, 1997; France, 1996). In 1980, unemployment amongst young people had grown 'by more than it had in the previous ten years put together' (MacDonald, 1997a: p. 20) and by the early 1990s the economic activity rate for young people had fallen drastically (Dean, 1997: p. 60). Young people experience twice the average rate of unemployment, and for 16–19 year olds, this stood at 20 per cent throughout the 1980s (France, 1996). So profound have these changes been that the labour market 'that now greets young women and men would have been unrecognisable thirty years ago' (MacDonald, 1997a).

Young people who do find work are five times more likely than older employees to be paid below half of male average earnings (JRF, 1998, q.v. Dean, 1997; Coles and Craig, 1999). In 1992, for instance, 16 and 17 year olds working full-time received just one third of the wages of full-time adult male workers (Dean, 1997). Under minimum wage legislation introduced by the New Labour government, young people aged under 21 are paid less than those who are over 21. The ethnicity and gender of the young person concerned, and the region in which they happen to live, additionally determine patterns of employment, unemployment and income levels. The chance of a young man in Sunderland being unemployed, for example, is three to one, while for a young man in St. Albans it is *thirty*-three to one (Ashton *et al.*, 1988, cited in Coles and Craig, 1999). Furthermore, young men from ethnic minority groups have consistently experienced higher rates of unemployment compared to their white counterparts (Coles and Craig, 1999). Research conducted in the mid-1980s demonstrated that there was 'undoubtedly an important and significant relationship between the problem of mass unemployment and Britain's new heroin problem' and suggested that 'it is futile to deny the links between unemployment and heroin' (Pearson, 1987).

Young People and Social Policy

In addition to the collapse of the youth labour market, a 'whole raft' of changes to social security regulations has undermined young people's entitlement to welfare benefits (Dean, 1997: p. 59). Since the 1980s and throughout the 1990s, young people's rights to receive income support and unemployment benefit have been significantly eroded (France, 1996; Dean, 1997; Coles and Craig, 1999). The 1988 Social Security Act, for example, removed the right to benefit for 16 and 17-year-olds and required them to undertake compulsory job training if they were not in education or employment (Dean, 1997). Even though there were not enough schemes to provide for all those who wanted them, benefit penalties were introduced for those who refused to take them up (Williamson, 1997; Dean, 1997). These limitations on entitlements were continued with the introduction of the Job Seeker's Allowance in 1996 and Labour's 'New Deal' arrangements (Theodore and Peck, 1999; Holden, 1999). As a result of these developments, in 1997 three-quarters of 16 and 17-year olds who were unemployed were without any income (JRF, 1998, q.v. France, 1996; Coles and Craig, 1999). The 1988 Act also reduced the level of benefits to which those aged 18–25 were entitled (Dean, 1997; Coles and Craig, 1999).

In addition to these changes, the government altered the way that hostel payments were made, to prevent those who were unemployed from living away from home (Dean, 1997). Age related housing benefits were introduced and the rights of those under 25 to receive such benefits have been curtailed (Dean, 1997; Coles and Craig, 1999). These changes in effect mean that young people's entitlement to welfare benefits is now biologically determined: they are assessed on the basis of chronological age rather than 'need' or financial obligations (Coles and Craig, 1999: p. 69). Andrews and Jacobs (1990: p. 74) have argued, that 'it is hard to escape the conclusion that young people have been deliberately selected as easy targets in the assault against benefits'.

Changes to education and the introduction of youth training schemes, combined with changes in the labour market and welfare rights, mean that a majority of young people currently stay in some form of education or training until they are past 16. Approximately 30 per cent now enter university (Parker *et al.*, 1998, q.v. Coles and Craig, 1999). In 1974 approximately 28 per cent of young people stayed in school for some form of further education, but by 1994 this had risen to 57 per cent (MacDonald, 1997a). Changes to the grant system and the introduction of student loans and tuition fees, however, mean that the average (educational) debt of young people aged 17–21 is £1,548 while for those aged 22–26 the figure increases to over £4,000 (France, 1996). These changes in the labour market, in entitlements to benefits and in education and training schemes have coincided with changes in the housing market. As a result of a decline in public sector housing, on one hand, and rising rents and reductions in housing benefits on the other, young people are less able to access affordable housing than they were in previous years (Coles and Craig, 1999, q.v. Dean, 1997; Pitts, 1997; Douglas and Gilroy, 1994).

The changes discussed above have been taking place at the same time as family structures themselves have become more 'brittle' (Coles and Craig, 1999). The predictable consequence of these changes, combined with, for example, changes to the public care system and the closure of children's homes, has been a phenomenal rise in levels of homelessness amongst the young (Coles and Craig, 1999; Douglas and Gilroy, 1994; Pitts, 1997).

The cumulative effects of these changes have been to make it impossible for some young people to make the transition to adult status. It is increasingly difficult for young people to establish independent homes and families of their own because they do not have the means to do so (Pitts, 1999; McLaughlin and Glendenning, 1994). Parker and colleagues (1998: p. 24) argue that by the age of 24–25 only half of young people have achieved economic autonomy and whereas about 75 per cent of 16–19-year-olds would still be living in the parental home a decade ago, recent research suggests it is now over 90 per cent.

The changes discussed here have also made it more likely that young people will engage in a range of legitimate or illegitimate informal economic activities provided by 'alternative opportunity structures' (Craine, 1997). These range from the quasi-legal (begging, engagement in the sex industry) at one end to the illegal (Dean and Melrose, 1996; Dean, 1997; Craine, 1997; Coles and Craig, 1999; Dean and Melrose, 1999; Melrose *et al.*, 1999; Melrose, 2000). In these activities we witness young people's creative, although sometimes self-destructive, attempts to respond to their structurally disadvantaged position (Melrose, 2000; Melrose *et al.*, 1999; Pitts, 1997; Craine, 1997; Blackman, 1997; Collison, 1996).

Vulnerable or Disadvantaged Youth

The discussion so far has established that in the contemporary social world, where global 'market society' prevails, the process of achieving economic and domestic autonomy has become extended, and more complex, for all young people. They are caught in a pincer movement between the demands of international capital on the one side and welfare retrenchment on the other (Melrose, 2000). For 'status-zero' youth, like those who took part in this study (i.e. those who are not in any form of education, work or training and who have no independent income (Williamson, 1997)) the transition to adulthood is 'fractured' as well as extended. That is, these young people may leave education or training without obtaining employment, or may leave the parental home or local authority care services without having a home of their own to go to (Coles and Craig, 1999, Pitts, 1997). These were the sort of young people who took part in this study. Most were without any qualifications or employment and many were living in hostels.

It is these groups, who, (if they are lucky) constitute the 'Macdonald's proletariat' (Lash, 1994: p. 120, cited in Collison, 1996: p. 429) of contemporary Britain. They are very often young and non-white. They comprise what IBM described as 'the peripherals': low skilled workers who can be pulled in and pushed out of the economy as and when they are required. This is not to suggest that such young people are merely the passive victims of economic forces or that they constitute an 'underclass' (Murray, 1990). These young people have 'choices but not choices over choices' (Willis 1990: p. 159 cited in Craine, 1997: p. 137). When they cannot find work they may beg, they may become engaged in the sex industry or they may buy and sell drugs. Some in fact might say that they prefer to do these things than to perform unrewarding work in the formal economy (Melrose *et al.*, 1999; Melrose, 2000). Their choices, however, are 'structured choices' (Pettiway, 1997: p. xxix; Pitts, 1997). Despite their disadvantaged positions, many of the young people who took part in this study remained attached to mainstream values: that is, they wanted homes, jobs and families of their own (c.f. Dean and Melrose, 1996; Dean and Melrose, 1999; Jones, 1997; Blackman, 1997).

'Gary'

Gary, for example, was a sixteen-year-old, living in a hostel when we met. He had offended and been excluded from school. He had begun smoking cigarettes and cannabis when he was ten and drinking alcohol when he was thirteen. At the time of the interview he continued to use cannabis although he had practically given up cigarettes and rarely drank alcohol. He was asked if he thought that he might stop using cannabis in the future:

> G. *Yeah, I will eventually.*
> M. *And what do you think might help you to do that?*
> G. *I think I'll just stop, when I start working and get a job and things like that.*

'Jane'

Jane, a seventeen-year-old who had also offended and been excluded from school and was also living in a hostel when we met. In the month before our conversation, she had used cannabis, speed, ecstasy and cocaine. She thought she would probably stop taking drugs when she had children and was clear that she wanted her children to have a better life than she had experienced:

> *I don't want my kids to do drugs. I'm gonna tell my kids, when they're old enough to know, I'm gonna tell them how many drugs I've done and how I fucked my life and I'll say to them, 'If you do the same I'll kill ya' (laughs) 'cos I don't want my kids turning out like me. I fucked up my life, I'm trying to make it good now, but I don't want my kids turning out like me.*

Jane had left home at the time of her GCSEs and consequently had not passed any exams. She said:

> *If I could go back to school again I would go back and do my GCSEs. I regret not doing them because like I've had jobs, yeah, but I've got no qualifications. I've tried a month at college. I got kicked out 'cos I kept going in stoned and bunking off to go and get stoned. I messed it up for myself but I don't expect no sympathy from anyone because I messed up.*

Such young people are of course 'active in the construction of their own history, but not as they please and not under circumstances of their own choosing' (Craine, 1997: p. 137). Their reduced circumstances tend to produce what has been described as a 'highly constrained agency' (Pitts, 1997; Melrose *et al.*, 1999). As a result of this, these young people tend to follow lifestyles that are 'inimical to their best interests' (Pitts, 1997) and inclined to reproduce their exclusion (from the school, the labour market, the family etc.), an exclusion which is (wrongly) understood to be their own fault (Collison, 1996: p. 429).

It has been suggested that young people who use drugs, but who are not as vulnerable as the young people who took part in this study, are able to sustain 'diverse narratives of self' (Giddens, 1991: p. 54, cited in Collison, 1996: p. 433). That is, they may go to raves and take drugs at weekends but on Monday morning can return to their 'normal' roles in work, education and families (Collison, 1996; Parker *et al.*, 1998). For these young people, drug taking appears to represent a means by which they may 'take time out' from the 'normal' pressures of everyday life (Parker *et al.*, 1998).

Vulnerable young people, however, may find that they do not have the agility to move between lifestyle sectors in the way that their not-so-vulnerable, drug using peers do because they have *already* been excluded, or excluded themselves, from school, work and families (Collison, 1996: p. 436). Moreover, these young people have often internalised images of themselves as 'bad' or 'stupid' or even 'worthless' (see Blackman, 1997). As a result of their exclusion from the lifestyle sectors in which their less vulnerable drug-using peers may engage (work, education and families) these young people often have nothing to take 'time out' from. In this context, drug use may move from being 'recreational' to 'entrenched'. 'Hustling' for drugs may become a way of meaningfully structuring time in lives that are unstructured by the temporal demands of formal work (Pearson, 1987). There may be economic advantages gained from 'hustling' (Pettiway, 1997; Bourgois, 1996). Alternatively, it may be that in these circumstances, drugs 'win by default'; as Burroughs has noted, 'you become a narcotics addict because you do not have strong motivations in any other direction' (Burroughs, 1977: p. 15).

For young people whose social, emotional and economic landscapes are not all that they might wish, 'street' or drug cultures might provide an arena in which they may feel they 'belong'. A study of juveniles who had become involved in prostitution showed that a sense of 'belonging' was important in keeping many of them involved (Melrose *et al.*, 1999). 'Street cultures' appeared to offer these young people, and those involved in begging (Dean and Melrose, 1999) a degree of certainty and security through which many of the uncertainties associated with being young and marginalised in contemporary society were neutralised (Collison, 1996). It is important to recognise, as Pitts (1997: p. 149) has pointed out, that when we are talking about disadvantaged young people, be it those who drift into prostitution or those who develop problematic levels and patterns of drugs use, 'those relationships and networks that might ordinarily serve to prevent their drift into self-destructive or self-defeating behaviour are absent and, to this extent, they are socially isolated'.

It may also be that for marginalised and disadvantaged young people, drugs assume a greater importance than they do in 'mainstream' youth culture. Symbolically, drugs may provide a means to reject the adult society from which these young people have already been excluded. On the other hand, using drugs may allow these young people to feel 'ordinary' in the sense that they are participating in activities that appear to be regarded as 'normal' by many of their less vulnerable peers. In the context of social deprivation 'drugs may provide a palliative to poor quality of life' (Hough, 1996). They may provide a means of 'escape' from the routine pressures of everyday life. In short, using drugs may fulfil a range of different functions for these young people. Additionally, or alternatively, drugs may provide these young people with a source of (street) cultural capital (Collison, 1996; Bourgois, 1996; Davis with Ruddick, 1988; ACMD, 1998), a certain amount of 'respect' (Bourgois, 1996; ACMD, 1998) and even a form of economic enterprise (Bourgois, 1996; Davis with Ruddick, 1988; ACMD, 1998). Drug markets may enable these young people to insert themselves into the global economy in ways that their formal skills (or lack of them) would not allow them (Bourgois, 1996; Davis with Ruddick, 1988). Vulnerable young people may derive a feeling of 'success' and therefore 'respect' from being able successfully to negotiate these markets. A respect that the edifice of inequality and requirements of the formal labour market deny them (Bourgois, 1996).

Conclusion

The discussion above has suggested that drug taking, especially the use of cannabis and ecstasy, is fairly widespread among many sections of 'youth' in contemporary society and that this phenomenon in itself may be related to the social and economic context in which young people now make their journey to adulthood. The following chapter introduces the young people who took part in the study and considers the possible relationships between 'vulnerability' and drug use by exploring the chronology of events between their experiences of:

- offending
- being excluded from school
- being looked after
- beginning to use drugs

This will enable us to investigate the extent to which their status as young offenders, school excludees and young people who have been looked after, places them at greater risk of drug use, and developing drug misuse problems, than their less vulnerable peers. We then go on to consider the backgrounds from which the young people had come and their current living situations.

Chapter 3

The Young People: Complexities in the Relationship Between Vulnerability and Drug Use

Introduction

The young people who took part in this study are amongst those identified by previous research as most 'vulnerable' to developing problems of drug misuse:

- young offenders
- young people excluded from school
- young people who had been looked after in the local authority care system

Other similarly 'vulnerable' groups are:

- the young homeless
- young people who have been sexually abused or exploited through their involvement in prostitution
- young people with alcohol or drug misusing parents
- young people with mental health problems

This chapter:

- introduces the young people who took part in the study
- looks at their present living circumstances
- considers a number of possible relationships between 'vulnerability' and drug use as a result of:
    - offending
    - exclusion from school
    - being looked after

The Young People

34 young men and 15 young women aged between 13–18, and six men and four women aged 19–25 took part in this study. The analysis looks primarily at the

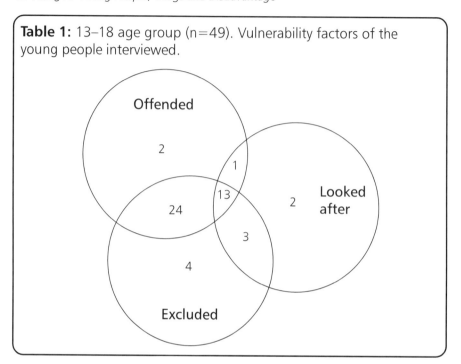

Table 1: 13–18 age group (n=49). Vulnerability factors of the young people interviewed.

49 13–18 year olds, as they are considered to be 'children' by the *Children Act (1989)* and the UN Convention on the Rights of the Child. The majority were white, just twelve participants were from ethnic minority groups, six of these were from mixed parentage, and six were from African-Caribbean communities. All these young people had offended, been excluded from school and/or looked after by local authority care services (see Table 1). They were contacted through Youth Offending Teams (YOTs), Pupil Referral Units (PRUs) and Youth Services in two local authority areas in the South-east of England and a small group was contacted in an inner London borough.

The young people were questioned about:

- Their experiences of:
  - family life and education
  - offending
  - being excluded from school
  - being looked after
- Their drug use
  - their reasons for taking them

- how they were introduced to them
- how they managed to access and pay for them
- what drugs they had taken
- what age they began to take drugs
- how they perceived their drug use
- what service interventions they thought might usefully help them stop using drugs
- Their consumption of:
  - alcohol
  - tobacco
  - and volatile substances

Many were already vulnerable, or potentially 'at risk' young people, as a result of the unstable family situations and the poverty of the communities from which they had come (HAS, 1996; Standing Conference on Drug Abuse (SCODA), 1997). If their offending, exclusion from school or being looked after rendered them 'vulnerable' to drug use, so many were already vulnerable as a result of these other factors. Although approximately half of the young people were too young to have any form of qualifications or to work on a full time basis, of those who were old enough, just four participants had some form of qualification and just three were in employment. Furthermore, many found themselves in insecure housing situations. Of those who were old enough to live independently of their families or carers, a quarter were living in hostels and a small group of five were staying with friends. Just five participants had their own flats that were either privately rented or in the public housing sector. Four participants were still living in the care of the local authority.

It was those who had offended, been excluded from school *and* been looked after (13) in local authority care whose housing and social and economic situations were the most insecure. Just one of them had qualifications and was in employment. Almost half of them were living in hostels or staying with friends. All the young people who were still in the care of the local authority were in this multi-disadvantaged group. These young people, whose experiences in terms of offending, exclusion from school and being looked after were clustered, also came from the most disorganised family backgrounds, had most frequently reported conflict or abuse in their families and most frequently reported parental drug use. The life experiences of these young people seems to have put them at greatest risk of developing drug problems. Before verifying whether in fact this was the case, it is necessary to consider some of the possible relationships between 'vulnerability' and drug use.

Drug Use and Vulnerability

As this was a qualitative study, the concern was to find out how the young people perceived the connections between their drug use, and their offending, exclusion from school or being looked after. Significantly, most of the young people did not appear to consider these things to be important in terms of their drug use. There were some exceptions to this, which will be discussed later, but generally, this was not a dominant theme. Indeed, thirteen participants were using drugs and many more were using alcohol and tobacco *before* the event which apparently put them at risk of beginning to use drugs, that is, *before* they had offended, been excluded from school or been looked after. It is important therefore to consider alternative ways of understanding the relationship between drug use and vulnerability by discussing some of these possible relationships and drawing on the voices and experiences of the young people themselves to illustrate the complexities of the processes involved.

The frequent use of the term 'career' to describe to a young person's experiences of offending, being excluded from school or being looked after indicates that each of these experiences is extremely complicated and may be associated with a lengthy process. Evidence suggests, for example, that a combination of incidents in the playground and classroom frequently precede the decision to exclude and young people may experience a number of exclusions (Martin *et al.*, 1999; OFSTED, 1996). The consequences of exclusion, the subsequent lack of education experienced by many young people, heightened family stress, fewer opportunities to remain in education and achieve qualifications, are potentially more damaging than the decision to exclude *per se* (Social Exclusion Unit, 1998).

Similarly, problems with parents, at school and in the community will typically precede entry into care (Triseliotis *et al.*, 1995) and the majority of young people entering the care system are known to present a number of very serious problems (Berridge and Brodie, 1998). Again, several care episodes may be experienced for varying amounts of time and the type of care placement may also be significant. In relation to young offenders, the type of offending may increase or decrease and the nature of the offences become more or less serious (Graham and Bowling, 1995). Additionally, young people may be involved in nuisance behaviour or offending without being caught.

The task of identifying the relationship between each of these experiences and drug taking is extremely complex and it is therefore important to avoid any suggestion that the relationship between drug use and the sorts of vulnerabilities being discussed here is simply a matter of 'cause and effect'.

As we have seen above, the experiences through which these young people were rendered 'vulnerable' to developing problems in relation to drug use did not fit into discrete 'categories' and there are complex overlaps between them. Equally, there did not appear to be a specific chronology or sequencing of events between exclusion from school, offending or being looked after and beginning to use drugs. Amongst those who had offended, been excluded from school *and* looked after, for example, equal proportions had offended before being looked after or been excluded before being looked after. Similarly, some young people had already begun to use drugs *before* they had been subject to any of these processes while others had begun to use drugs *after* one or more of these events. This produces four possibilities.

1. To what extent is drug use a contributory factor to vulnerability?

Firstly then, it is important to think about the extent to which drug use was a contributory, or even the main reason, for a young person being looked after, excluded from school or offending. Although drug use is sometimes the reason for a young person being excluded from school (OFSTED, 1996), the majority of school exclusions are not drug-related (SCODA, 1997) and none of the people we spoke to had been excluded for this reason. Neither were any of these young people looked after as a direct result of drug use. Some participants, however, did have drug related convictions, that is, some had been convicted of offences of possessing drugs or of possession with intent to supply drugs, although these were not usually their first or only convictions.

'Carly'

Carly had been looked after *before* she had offended or been excluded from school, and began to use drugs *after* she first became looked after. She was fourteen when we met and still living in the care of the local authority. Carly came from a violent and abusive home. Her father was violent to her mother and Carly frequently went missing from home in her young life. When she was ten, Carly was placed in a children's home because her father had raped her older sister. She continued to go missing from the care placement. At eleven, Carly started using alcohol, tobacco and cannabis and stopped attending school. At twelve she was still running from care and began to use cocaine and ecstasy. She also became involved in offending at this age and was convicted for 'drugs, violence, burglary, robbery and shoplifting' between the ages of 12 and 13. At fourteen, still in the care of the local authority, Carly continued to use cocaine, she was 'getting drunk a lot' and would use volatile substances if she was unable to get cocaine. At the time of the interview, Carly was still using cannabis, cocaine and ecstasy 'whenever I can get them: about three times a week'. She was seeing a psychiatrist and was being prescribed temazepan apparently to help her stop using cocaine. She said she wanted to stop using cocaine so that she could return home to live with her mother but she was 'addicted to the buzz' and was finding it difficult to stop.

On the other hand, some participants admitted that they had committed offences in order to provide money with which to obtain drugs but again these were not normally their first or sole convictions.

'John'

John was an eighteen year old who had offended, been excluded from school and been looked after. He had started using cannabis when he was twelve and during his teenage years had been involved in offending behaviour. He was staying in a bail hostel when he was introduced to crack-cocaine. In order to finance his crack use he had committed more crimes. He said:

> You want it so badly, it's like in your mind, you don't, it's weird, you really do want it. Next time you haven't got it, then, that's when I went out and robbed someone...That's what I was doing every day to get it. I was smoking it every day.

This demonstrates that John's offending is '*drug-driven*' and directly related to his use of crack-cocaine but the relationship between his previous drug use and offending is much less clear. On the other hand Carly's crime is '*drug related*' (Hough, 1996, cited in Barton, 1999). That is, her crimes were not committed to finance drug use but she has a conviction for possession of drugs with intent to supply, amongst other things.

2. To what extent is drug use a precursor to vulnerability?

Secondly, there is the possibility that young people are using drugs *before* they are put at risk of drug misuse as a result of offending, exclusion from school or being looked after which suggests that some young people become vulnerable to drug use as a result of other influences or factors in their lives. This does not mean that these events are totally unconnected, but in order to establish any connections, the complexity of the processes that precede being looked after, offending or being excluded from school must be taken into account. Research with children looked after in residential care has shown, for example, that many young people are vulnerable to drug use *before* they become looked after. In one study, 40 per cent of 14–15-year-olds and 54 per cent of those over 15 had been offered cannabis *before* they were admitted to the home. It was clear from this study that many of the young people 'knew a lot about drugs' and drugs were widely available in the home (Sinclair and Gibbs, 1998). The authors concluded, however, that there was no evidence that 'the homes in themselves were an important source of recruitment to the drug 'culture' (Sinclair and Gibbs, 1998: p. 184).

'Gary'

Gary, a sixteen-year-old who had offended and been excluded from school, when he was fifteen and sixteen respectively, had started smoking cannabis when he was ten. The time lapse between Gary's first use of drugs, his offending behaviour and his exclusion from school, and the young age at which he had begun to use cannabis demonstrates that he was not vulnerable to drug use *as a result of* offending or exclusion from school. On the other hand, because he had started using cannabis at such a young age, he may have become more vulnerable to experiences of offending and exclusion from school.

3. Can drug taking and vulnerability be contemporaneous?

Thirdly, there is the possibility that drug taking and vulnerability collide. Being looked after, excluded from school and offending, are temporal *processes* rather than singular *events*. A young person may be looked after or involved in offending or behaviour that renders them vulnerable to exclusion from school and drug use for varying lengths of time. There may, therefore, be overlaps between the experience of these events and drug use.

'Susan'

Susan's case provides an illustration of the ways in which vulnerabilities and drug taking coincide. Susan was sixteen when she was interviewed and had been using cannabis since the age of eleven. She had been using alcohol and smoking from the age of nine. Susan had been sexually abused from the age of five and became looked after when she was fourteen as a consequence of this. When she was eleven (*after* she had first used drugs) Susan was first convicted of an offence and continued to offend after she became looked after. While she was being looked after she continued to use cannabis and began to use cocaine and ecstasy. When she was fifteen Susan was temporarily excluded from school and later in the same year was excluded permanently. Susan had left care at sixteen and, supported by the independent living team, was living in her own flat at the time of the interview. She continued to use cannabis, amphetamine, cocaine, ecstasy and LSD on a regular basis: that is, cannabis every day, amphetamines twice a week and cocaine, ecstasy or LSD at weekends.

'Jane'

Jane also provides an example of the ways in which such influences may collide. She had stopped attending school and had started using drugs *before* becoming involved in offending behaviour. She was seventeen and living in a hostel when we met. She said:

> *Umm, I got into trouble at school when I went to High school. They umm, like the high school I went to, they all like thought I'd be like my brother. My big brother, because like he was like all good at school an' that, and good grades, and he, they all thought I'd be the same but I weren't,* **so I tried making a point by being naughty.** *I didn't do any GCSEs.* (emphasis added)

Jane explained that she moved out of home for a month and stopped attending school:

> *…whilst GCSEs were going on and I was getting stoned and drunk everyday of that month…Whilst I was away from home I got arrested twice and then I got bailed and cautioned. I got two cautions.*

Jane had moved back home but things didn't work out between her and her mother:

> *So basically, this Christmas just gone, I moved out of home four days after Christmas to live with my now ex-boyfriend. We moved to Southend on New Year's Eve. We lived there for two weeks in like a bed and breakfast place then we went to Basildon for three months. In that three months I started doing a bit of drugs like cocaine, I done half a pill (ecstasy) which was the only pill I'd ever taken…I done more speed than I would normally and I was just like doing puff like solid an' that…So I was smoking solid and umm, I was taking cocaine, snorting cocaine and smoking it in a joint and I was smoking cigarettes and getting drunk, not working. I was just sleeping all the time and having, like, just being lazy not doing anything really.*

Jane said that, in the month before we had met, she had used cannabis, alcohol, tobacco, amphetamines, ecstasy and 'coke if it's offered'. She said she would use drugs 'whenever I can'.

4. Is vulnerability a precursor to drug use?

Fourthly, it is necessary to consider the extent to which being looked after, excluded from school or offending creates a situation in which the young person becomes vulnerable to drug use. The discussion has already shown that young people who are excluded from school and left without educational provision are more at risk of becoming involved in offending behaviour (Martin *et al.*, 1999). Similarly, one might speculate that a young person's behaviour may be affected by the experiences of entering the care system or the juvenile justice system where they may be exposed to new peer groups, and possibly, value systems. Previous research evidence has in fact suggested that young people living in children's homes often experience pressure from others to take drugs (Sinclair and Gibbs, 1998). Half the young people in this study had started using drugs *after* becoming vulnerable through offending, school exclusion and/or being looked after.

'John'

As mentioned before, John had offended, been excluded from school and been looked after before he had started using crack-cocaine, but he had started smoking cannabis when he was twelve: before he had experienced any of the events that made him vulnerable to drug use. Both his drug taking and his offending behaviour, however, escalated after the experience of being cared for and after he had entered the juvenile justice system. He had, after all, been living in a bail hostel when he was introduced to crack-cocaine and, after beginning to use crack, his offending behaviour became more frequent and more serious.

'Barry'

Barry, a fifteen-year-old, also demonstrates the ways in which vulnerabilities may escalate. He had stopped attending school *before* he had offended or been looked after and began to use drugs *after* all of these experiences. He had lived with his mum after his parents had divorced. When he was twelve, he was sent to live with his father. At thirteen, he returned to live with his mother, at this time he stopped attending school and was cautioned by the police for violent offences. At fourteen, Barry was placed in foster care. At this time he was cautioned for being drunk and disorderly but was not convicted. At fifteen, he began to use cannabis, ecstasy and amphetamine. His foster placement broke down and he returned to live with his mother. When we met, he was still living with his mother. He continued to use cannabis 'one or two times a week' and also used 'speed, E and Charlie' (cocaine) although 'not on a regular basis'.

Conclusion

Connected to the escalation of vulnerabilities is the question of whether different types of vulnerability are more or less significant in the initiation of drug using careers and the development of drug problems. This question is explored in subsequent chapters which look at what drugs these young people had used and the ages at which they had begun to use them to see if, indeed, it was those who:

- had offended
- been excluded from school and
- been looked after in local authority care

who were the most vulnerable to developing problematic patterns of drug use.
Some case study examples of the young people's lives are given in Appendix 1.

Chapter 4

Motivations and Pathways:
The Why and How of Drug Use

Introduction

This chapter examines what the young people said about:
- why they had started using drugs
- how they were introduced to and accessed drugs
- how they were able to afford drugs

Why Did the Young People Start Using Drugs?

When the young people were asked specifically about why they had started using drugs their motivations for doing so could be classified in five different ways:

1. oblivion seeking
2. acceptance seeking
3. thrill seeking
4. seeking thrills *and* acceptance
5. seeking oblivion *and* acceptance.

1. Oblivion seeking

Some of the young people said they had begun to use drugs in order to escape from other problems in their lives, for example, family conflict and abuse. These were classified as 'oblivion seekers' and represent approximately a fifth of the young people who took part in the study.

'Steven'

Steven, for example, was seventeen at the time of the interview. He had offended and been excluded from school and had experienced a difficult home life. He had also been sexually abused when he was nine by someone outside the family. When he was sixteen, Steven's parents divorced and he left home. At this time, he had started using cannabis, LSD, amphetamines and ecstasy. He was also 'just experimenting' with crack-cocaine and heroin for a period of about three months. He told us:

> It [crack and heroin] *was like a mental crutch to block out all the bad stuff.*

'Cassie'

Similarly, Cassie had experienced physical and mental abuse at the hands of her step-father. She told us she had started using heroin when she was fifteen in order to:

> *...block out all the, like, things that had happened to me in the past, mm, just like to really forget about it...I had like a lot of problems in my family and, it started off with my mum and dad's divorce and then my mum got a new boyfriend and I didn't get on with him and the stuff he used to do to me I didn't want to remember...A few of us were all just sat around having a laugh and a joke, chatting an' that, and they all knew that I had like a really bad past so my ex-boyfriend said 'Do you want to give this a go? I'll give you a little bit to start with and see how you like it, if you don't then we won't do any more'. He said 'it will just put you on a bit of a high so you can forget about it' and I thought, 'yeah, great, if I can forget my problems, then yeah, go for it'...I thought it was something to block out all the problems an' that's how I see it, it was something to block out problems and then it started to make me worse and that's when I realised it wasn't to help my problems, it was making them worse.*

It is interesting that both these young people use the term 'block out' when they explain why they had started using drugs. It is obvious that in this context drug use represents a form of self-medication and personal attempts to cope with problems (albeit by blocking them out) rather than any form of hedonistic self-indulgence.

2. Acceptance seeking

Approximately a quarter of participants said they had started using drugs because all their friends were doing so, or because everyone they knew was using drugs. For this group, 'fitting in' with their peers seemed to be especially important and they have been described as 'acceptance seekers'.

'Lee'

Lee, for example, a young offender who was fourteen at the time of the interview said he had started using cannabis after he went to a new school:

> ...*peer pressure, went to a new school, got some mates who were smoking it* [weed], *then hash, then I started getting this buzz so I just kept on.*

'Paul'

Similarly, Paul said:

> *I was hanging around in a big group, you watch them do it then you want to. Like, peer pressure, and like, trying to be like them. You just try it and then you think, 'yeah'. You want to be one of them really, don't you? So you think, 'Yeah, I'll try some'.*

It is interesting that both these participants use the term 'peer pressure'. This term suggests that, for some young people, conformity to peer group norms is experienced as a form of coercion.

'Michael'

Michael, however, talked of a different form of peer influence when he spoke about how he had started using volatile substances:

> *Well, I was just like going down the road and my mate's sitting there sniffing and I was like, 'What's that?' I was a teenager, I was thirteen, and he goes, 'Oh it's lighter fluid, do you want to try some?' He like showed me how to do it an' that and I tried lighter gas an' I liked it. And then like petrol and then I took some more on a different day and then it all started off to be, 'Oh, go and get some gas, oh, here we are, here's £1.50, get me a can as well', whatever. And then it really started. The most I've, the worst period of me sniffing was between the ages of 15 and 16, cos I got put inside* [a secure unit] *just before I was 16.*

Clearly, for this group, gaining acceptance from peers is an important element in the decision to use drugs. It may be that such acceptance from friends and associates becomes all the more important when young people are removed from situations that provide 'normal' opportunities for extending peer networks. Being excluded from school, being moved from the area in which one might have grown up in order to be looked after in local authority care, or being removed to a young offenders' institution, for example, might disrupt already established peer associations. In such circumstances, a young person might feel the 'pressure' to belong to a new peer group even more acutely. On the other hand, already established peer groups may have led the young person to take drugs in the first place, as in the case of Paul. Where these peer groups are disrupted, it may be that the young person feels the need to remain involved with them even more intensely and will do whatever it takes in order to do so. Additionally, or alternatively, the sense of uncertainty and dislocation that is generated in the contemporary social context may make the need for security derived from the feeling that one is 'accepted' even more profound.

3. Thrill seeking

Approximately a fifth of the young people said that they had started using drugs because they were curious about the effects and because they wanted a 'buzz'. These have been classified as 'thrill seekers'.

'Pete'

Pete had not attended school since the age of six, but had instead received home tuition. He had started using cannabis when he was about thirteen because he was 'curious' about it. When he was fourteen, he was offered some crack, and, he said:

> I didn't know anything about drugs so I tried it because I wanted to know what it was like.

Also when he was fourteen he was offered some heroin and his curiosity had led him to try injecting it. He said he had only tried it once and had not done it again because he 'didn't like injections'. He had, however, continued to use crack-cocaine about three times a week for a period of two years. When he was interviewed, Pete said he had not used any crack for the past nine months.

'Alan'

Alan was seventeen at the time of the interview. He had offended and been excluded from school and had started using cannabis when he was thirteen. Alan had recently started using 'acid' (LSD) and said that he took it about once a month when he was going to 'raves'. Alan thought 'acid' was:

> A pukka buzz. That's what it's about, getting a buzz.

'Carly'

Similarly, Carly said that after initially trying drugs she had continued to use them because:

> *I like the buzz. It makes me feel confident to do things.*

Carly also said that she preferred the 'buzz' she got from drugs, to the 'buzz' she got from alcohol and it was because 'I'm addicted to the buzz' that she found it difficult to stop using cocaine.

For this group of 'thrill seekers', drug taking does clearly represent a form of hedonistic indulgence. It may be that in the circumstances of a mundane and largely unrewarding everyday life, drug taking offers a sense of excitement that is not available through other avenues.

4. Thrill and acceptance seeking

Approximately another fifth of the young people said they had started taking drugs because all their friends were and because they were curious about the effects, or they wanted to see what the 'buzz' was like. This group has been described as 'thrill *and* acceptance seekers'.

'Jane'

Jane, who had started using drugs to make herself appear more grown up in front of her older boyfriend, also said:

> *I'm the sort of person who likes living on the edge. I like danger. I get a thrill out of the fact that I might die, and the fact of, oh, doing naughty things and that. I get a thrill out of it. I don't know why, it's weird, it's prob…some people might say I'm sick and twisted for thinking like that but I get a thrill out of it* [laughs]. *You know what I mean? It adds a spice to my everyday life* [laughs] *makes it less boring.*

This group is clearly concerned with both acceptance from peer groups as well as hedonistic indulgence. In Jane's case, for instance, drugs seemed to promise some, otherwise lacking, excitement in her life as well as a means of signalling her 'maturity' to her older boyfriend.

5. Oblivion and acceptance seeking

A small group of five participants have been classified as 'oblivion and acceptance seekers'. This group said they had started using drugs to escape from other problems, *and* because all their friends were using drugs.

'Beth'

Beth fell into this category. When she was asked why she had started using drugs she said:

> It was the only way I knew. My mum and all her friends were using and they encouraged me and at eleven, I thought it was cool. It was also a way out of all the grief.

'Carl'

Carl, who had been placed in the care of the local authority by his step-father after his mother had died said:

> When I went into care, that's when I took drugs and started drinking... I started drinking a lot, drinking and smoking. Just after I went into care...I'd never tried anything before that.

Carl remained vulnerable to drug use after he left the care system:

> Well I moved in with my auntie after I moved out of care and she used to deal drugs so I was around a lot of drug dealers and things like that so I used to take a lot of drugs with them. Most everyday and then it was LSD as well.

For this group, clearly, escape from previous problems, as well as the perception that drug use is 'normal' or that 'everybody does it', are significant elements in their decision to use drugs. It may be that using drugs to escape from problems appears 'normal' when one's friends (or in Beth and Carl's case, family) are also using drugs and apparently 'escaping' from the mundane reality of everyday life.

Vulnerability, Age and Motivation

'Oblivion seekers', 'acceptance seekers', 'thrill seekers', 'acceptance and thrill seekers' and 'oblivion and acceptance seekers' were fairly evenly distributed across the different vulnerable groups identified. Particular motivations for initiating drug use were not confined to any specific group. However, when comparison is made across the different *age* cohorts it would seem that motivations for initiating drug use appear to be quite different. Just one person in the older age group had initiated drug use because they appeared to be seeking 'acceptance' compared to a quarter of the younger age group. Similarly, just one person in the older age group had initiated drug use because they appeared to be seeking 'oblivion', compared to a fifth of the younger age cohort. 'Thrill seeking' seemed to be a much more important reason for initiating drug use in the older age group than it was in the younger group.

The evidence indicates that these young people had begun to use drugs for a variety of, often complex, reasons. There was no simple or direct correlation, for example, between offending, exclusion from school and being looked after and motivations for beginning to use drugs. In order to understand why young people begin to use drugs it would appear to be necessary to view the young person holistically and to look at the background and circumstances of the individual child. It is also important to look at the ways in which that young person interacts with its social environment, for example, in the family and in peer groups. Understanding rather than assuming motivations for drug use is important for all those working with, or involved in caring for, young people. Different motivations for using drugs will of course require different responses. It is important, in practice, when thinking about ways to respond to the problems these young people present, that intervention strategies are linked to their motivations for beginning to use, and/or continuing to use, drugs.

How Did the Young People Become Involved in Drug Use?

This section explores the mechanisms through which young people were introduced to drugs and the means by which they were able to access both illicit drugs and licit substances such as alcohol and volatile substances. What young people said about how they managed to pay for the drugs they consumed is also examined.

For the most part, these young people had been introduced to drugs and other substances through their friends and peer groups and, on a small number of occasions, by relatives such as cousins, siblings or aunts and uncles. This finding is common to other studies of young people and substance use which have shown that 'peer groups and peer clusters are invariably the means through which young people are introduced to drugs' (ACMD, 1998; Lloyd *et al.*, 1998). Other evidence has suggested that peer group associations may be especially important in the lives of young people who are vulnerable (Farmer and Pollock, 1998; Otero-Lopez *et al.*, 1994). They have been shown, for example, to be a significant feature in the lives of young people who become involved in prostitution (Melrose *et al.*, 1999).

'Paul'

Paul described the circumstances in which he had decided to start using drugs and demonstrates the significance of peer influences in this process:

> *I was with my mates, like the same group of mates I've hung around with for most of my life, so that's what made it, like, made me try it even more. 'Cos like they're proper mates, that at the time were doing it, so I thought, 'Well yeah, if they can do it, I'll do it'.*

'Beth'

On the other hand, Beth, a seventeen-year-old who had offended, been excluded from school and looked after, gave a particularly disturbing account of the way in which her mother and aunts introduced her to drugs. Beth's mother was a cocaine addict and had regularly injected drugs in front of Beth from when she was 'about eight'. Her mother, who was divorced from Beth's father, would also take Beth out regularly at this age to visit friends who were 'all doing drugs'. At the same time, her mother kept Beth off school in order to take her shoplifting with her. Beth had started using alcohol, tobacco and cannabis when she was 'about eight' and, for her eleventh birthday, her mother gave her an ecstasy tablet. Beth used 'speed' (amphetamines) between the ages of eleven and fourteen. At fourteen, her aunt gave Beth her first intravenous injection (of methadone) and, from fourteen to sixteen, she used heroin and cocaine intravenously. On her sixteenth birthday Beth attempted suicide but was unsuccessful in her attempt to kill herself. She was taken to hospital and from there referred to a psychiatrist. With the help of a social worker and a youth justice worker, Beth was able to stay off drugs and move away from the area in which she had grown up. At the time of the interview she continued to use cannabis but claimed not to have used any other drugs in the past year. Beth also had a history of sexual abuse.

In Beth's case, it is evident that the factors that had made her vulnerable to initiating drug use were the very same factors that had made her vulnerable to offending, being excluded from school and being looked after. Her vulnerability clearly derives from the family circumstances and local environment in which she found herself. Beth's case demonstrates the complexity of the factors involved in beginning to use drugs and the severity of the difficulties some of these young people have faced in their lives. Her case demonstrates that unravelling the causal chain of events between vulnerability as a result of offending, exclusion from school or being looked after and beginning to use drugs is an extremely difficult task.

How young people had been introduced to drugs did not vary significantly across the vulnerable groups. However, in some cases, especially where vulnerabilities were compounded, the circumstances of offending, being looked after and being excluded from school were important influences in the decision to use drugs.

'Michael'

Michael, for example, said:

> I was in a children's home, and umm, somebody said to me, 'Oh, here, you drink, you sniff (gas and glue), you smoke cigarettes, there's something else you ought to try'. And, the next stage up, sort of thing, so I was watching him and had a spliff and that, an' he was showing me how to do it like.

'Carl'

Similarly, Carl, who was eighteen at the time of the interview, had started using cannabis at twelve and then began using LSD, ecstasy and amphetamines. His mother had died when he was twelve and he was placed in the care of the local authority by his step-father. He said:

> When I went into care, that's when I took drugs and started drinking...because there was no-one, no authority from any one.

There is some evidence that young offenders and young people who are excluded from school tend to associate with older peers and some of the young people we spoke to had been introduced to drugs through their associations with older friends.

'Jane'

Jane, for example, a seventeen-year-old who had offended and been excluded from school, had been introduced to both drugs and crime at fourteen by an older boyfriend. She demonstrates that associating with older peers is sometimes important in a young person's decision to initiate drug use.

> I just wanted to make myself older before my time, really, if you know what I mean. I wanted to grow up before it was my time, I just liked it [cannabis] really, and I thought, 'Why not?'

For some young people, therefore, the circumstances of offending, being out of school or being looked after in local authority care, allows them to become involved in peer groups that provide opportunities for using drugs. Those involved in working with vulnerable young people therefore need to be aware of the peer networks in which young people are involved and, where possible, provide opportunities through which they might develop positive peer group associations. Peer mentoring schemes have been shown to be effective in other work with young people (Department of Health, 1996) and may prove an effective strategy to employ in this context.

How Did the Young People Access Drug Markets?

As we saw in Chapter 1, the drugs many of these young people have used had been illegal since before many of them were born. Since 1985, it has been illegal to sell solvents and other volatile substances to people under eighteen where it is suspected that such substances will be used for the purpose of intoxication. It is also illegal to sell tobacco products to people under the age of sixteen and alcohol to people under eighteen. The law, however, appeared to present no barrier to the young people who took part in this study. Of those who had used volatile substances, over three-quarters had first done so before they were fourteen. Similarly, over three-quarters had started smoking before they were fourteen and just less than three-quarters had first used alcohol before this age. When Paul was asked if he had ever had any difficulties in gaining access to drugs, he said:

> Not puff, never had a problem with puff. Glue and gas, 'cos I used to nick deodorants, nick the air fresheners, umm, and, er, with lighter gas I used to hang about outside Kwik-Save and ask someone, 'Can you go to the shop for me please?' 'What do you want?' 'A can of lighter fluid, it's for my mum'. Some people would do it, some wouldn't.

Similarly, Tony, a seventeen-year-old African-Caribbean who had offended and been excluded from school, had first used alcohol when he was fourteen. He said:

> Even at that age I used to get served in the local off-licence.

As well as illegal access to these licit substances, these young people also had access to a wide range of illicit substances, in spite of their young age. Sam, for example, had started smoking cannabis when he was thirteen, and he was asked about how he obtained drugs:

> Q. Did you find it quite easy to come across drugs? Did you have any difficulty getting hold of them?
> S. No.
> Q. How did you manage to get hold of them?

S. *Just the right person, really. They'd come down the shops everyday and say, 'blah, blah, blah, do you want this or do you want that?' We'd go round the back of the shops and get our money out and then like, he'd dish out the drugs.*

Paul, whose peers tended to be older than him, said:

Mostly my mates used to get them for me 'cos, like, they were a lot older than I was.

It is fairly clear from this discussion that drugs are widely available in the neighbourhoods and environments from which these young people come. As Pitts (2001) and Pearson (1987, cited in Pitts, 2001) have argued, in neighbourhoods that are 'de-stabilised' as a result of unemployment, poor housing, family poverty and the clustering of other sorts of social and economic disadvantage, 'connections into crime' and 'connections into drugs are' closely associated. From these environments arises 'a vociferous demand for other sources of solace' and drugs step in to fill 'a pressing social and economic need' (Pitts, 2001).

If gaining access to drug markets did not present these young people with any difficulties, paying for drugs sometimes did. We heard earlier from John who said that he had been 'robbing people' in order to finance his use of crack-cocaine. Other young people also said they had resorted to crime in order to pay for the drugs they were using. Carl, for instance, said:

Sometimes I robbed places. Houses, shops. I don't, I'm not, I don't actually, I'm not the sort of person who does that to get money. I'd rather go out and just beat someone up.

Similarly, Tommy told us:

I used to do burglaries and that. I was doing burglaries and that, like, an' then I thought to myself, 'It ain't worth it'.

Those who said they had financed their drug taking through crime were a minority of those who took part in the study. When young people had been involved in offending behaviour, this was often unrelated to their drug use. Some participants said they used their pocket money to 'chip in' with friends to buy drugs and some said they could get drugs 'on tick' if they were unable to pay for them immediately. It is possible of course that some young people were selling drugs to other friends and acquaintances in order to pay for their own drug use although none of them explicitly acknowledged as much.

For many young women who develop drug problems, the sex industry of course may provide opportunities through which the desired income might be generated (Melrose *et al.*, 1999; Melrose, 2000; May *et al.*, 2000). Two young women (who were friends), one of whom was 21, and the other who was 18, had been using crack-cocaine regularly, combined with heroin occasionally. They said they had been involved in prostitution in order to obtain money for drugs. Studies of young people who become involved in prostitution have in fact shown that this is not uncommon (O'Neill *et al.*, 1995; Melrose *et al.*, 1999; May *et al.*, 2000). When we met, the older of these women was pregnant and living in a hostel. Her friend had a rented flat. The young woman who was pregnant had stopped using crack as a result of concern for her baby. She was looking forward to having the baby, however, so that after it was born she could have 'one last binge' (on crack). She said that after this 'last binge' she would stop using drugs and care for her baby. The other woman, however, had used crack in the month before the interview and told us she used it 'every time I get the money'. Both women said they were no longer involved in prostitution when they were interviewed.

Conclusion

This section has demonstrated that illicit substances are widely available in the areas in which these young people have grown up and that the law appears to present no barriers to gaining access to either licit or illicit substances. Such barriers are more often financial, rather than legal or social. This places a responsibility on the police to enforce laws in relation to juvenile access to alcohol, cigarettes and volatile substances and to make every effort to reduce the availability of illicit drugs on the streets (President of the Council, 1998).

Chapter 5

Patterns of Youthful Drug Use: The What and When of Drug Use

Introduction

This chapter examines:
- the specific drugs used by the young people
- the ages at which they had begun to consume different drugs
- the patterns of drug use that they had developed
- their perceptions of their drug use

What Drugs Did These Young People Use?

A small group of five participants had never used or tried any illicit substances. Within the drug-using group, three distinct groups could be identified: those who only used cannabis, those who used cannabis in conjunction with other drugs and those who used cannabis in conjunction with other drugs and volatile substances.

The non-drug users

The small group of five participants who had never used illicit substances is looked at first because, although small in number, this group indicates that vulnerability as a result of offending, exclusion from school and being looked after does not *inevitably* lead to illicit drug use. This group is therefore important in the context of the whole discussion.

These non-drug users were dispersed across the vulnerable groups: two had offended and been excluded from school; one had offended, been excluded from school and looked after; one had been excluded from school and looked after; while another had only been looked after. These young people were also distributed across age groups: two were 16–17; one was 15–16; one was 14–15; and one

13–14. Their non-drug use, therefore, cannot be interpreted as simply a function of their age. This group also came from a range of family backgrounds, two were from reconstituted families, one was from a single parent household, one was from a nuclear family and one was from a family where the parents had divorced. In this sense, their backgrounds and experiences of offending, being excluded from school and being looked after render them as vulnerable as other participants to initiating drug use. Although this group did not use illicit substances, they all smoked cigarettes and three of the five used alcohol. None of this group had ever tried or used volatile substances.

Those who had never used illegal drugs tended to regard drug taking and the people who took drugs as 'just stupid'. Colin, for instance, a thirteen-year-old who had offended and been excluded from school, said:

> They're [drugs] a waste of money. They muck up your head and your life. I can't see any point in it.

Similarly, Andy, a sixteen-year-old who had been excluded from school and looked after, told us he thought that people who use drugs were:

> Idiots. I don't see the point in it.

It was obviously difficult to talk to these young people about why they had *not* used drugs; anyone would find it difficult to articulate their reasons for *not* engaging in any particular activity if they had never considered doing so. Clearly, however, their views about drugs, and the people who use them, were at odds with their equally vulnerable, drug using peers and it is evident that this group has, in some way, been protected from the temptation to try drugs. Colin's view, for example, suggests that he considered the benefits that might derive from drug use not worth the price in terms of financial and health costs. In order to explore fully what had protected these young people from drug use a more in-depth analysis of their life histories and present circumstances would have been required which was unfortunately beyond the scope of this project. There is, however, an issue here to be investigated in future research.

The drug users

Amongst the drug users, three distinct patterns of use could be identified. All had used cannabis, but just ten participants, less than a quarter, had only *ever* used cannabis. On the other hand, approximately a third had used cannabis in conjunction with other drugs *and* volatile substances, whereas a similar proportion had used cannabis in conjunction with other drugs but had *not* used volatile substances. Once again, however, drug use patterns did not correlate strongly with any particular vulnerable group. Of those who used cannabis in conjunction with other drugs, or other drugs and volatile substances, the patterns of use followed fairly complex patterns. Overall, approximately two-thirds had used amphetamines, just over half had used cocaine, and just over a third had used crack-cocaine or LSD or heroin.

Among this group of drug-using young people, there were variations in both the level and frequency of their use of cannabis and other drugs as might be expected of course, depending on what drugs are being talked about (Shiner and Newburn, 1997). While a majority admitted that they used cannabis on a daily basis, some said they would smoke just 'one or two spliffs a day' while others said they might smoke eight or more. For the most part, their use of *other* drugs (e.g. amphetamine, cocaine, ecstasy, LSD, heroin etc.) was more infrequent and again levels and frequency of use varied. Some told us they took amphetamines 'once or twice a week' while others said they would tend to use drugs such as amphetamine, ecstasy, cocaine and LSD at weekends or once a month. Recreational use of these drugs at weekends tended to be associated with being with friends, going out and having 'fun'. In this these young people appear not to be so different from their less vulnerable drug using peers (q.v. Parker *et al.*, 1998). The more regular use of cannabis, on the other hand, tended to be associated with 'chilling out' or relaxing.

It is also important to distinguish between *lifetime prevalence* of drug use and drug use in the *immediate past*, because young people's use of drugs is inclined to be highly 'fluid' (ACMD, 1998) and tends to alter over time (Newburn, 1999; Measham *et al.*, 1998; Edmunds *et al.*, 1998). Consequently, measures of use in the past month, provide 'more reliable estimates of the extent of current or regular use' (Shiner and Newburn, 1997: p. 515). The young people were therefore asked about the drugs that they had *ever* used (lifetime prevalence) and the drugs they had used in the month before the interview (recent use).

There was considerable variation between lifetime prevalence rates and recent drug use (q.v. Newburn, 1999; Measham *et al.*, 1998; Edmunds *et al.*, 1998). Approximately two thirds had ever used cannabis in conjunction with volatile substances or other drugs, but just over a quarter said that they had used this combination of substances in the month before the interview. Further, although just five participants said they had *never* used illicit drugs this figure had increased to eleven when they were asked about what drugs they had used recently. There are a number of ways in which the differences between lifetime prevalence and recent use might be interpreted.

The difference between lifetime prevalence of drugs and recent use

Firstly, some drugs more than others, appeared to be associated with the early stages of drug taking careers. Moving away from using these drugs (and perhaps onto others) is therefore a sign of 'maturity'. This was particularly the case in relation to volatile substance use. Michael, for example, a sixteen-year-old who had offended, been excluded from school and been looked after, had regularly used volatile substances, over a sustained period of time, since he was thirteen. He said he had taken so much gas that:

> *I could have been British gas!*

Michael said he had not used volatile substances for seven months prior to the interview because:

> *After I came out of the secure unit I went to a foster placement and sorted myself out.*

Michael also seemed concerned to signal his 'maturity' in relation to drug use when he said:

> *As I was saying, I sorted out my life and all I do is drink and puff and smoke cigarettes. And I don't see no problem with smoking puff, 'cos at the end of the day, I think that, like, people who sit there and will take it in a bong or just do it for the rush, they're kids. Like myself, I like to sit there and I roll it and I'll be relaxed when I smoke that. And I won't be sat there chuffing it and waiting to roll the next one, I'll be relaxed and sometimes it will take me about ten minutes to smoke one because I sit there and relax in front of the telly with a beer or whatever.*

There appeared to be quite a bit of this temporal distancing from what participants perceived as 'childish' behaviour associated with uncontrolled use in early adolescence to a more controlled, and 'sensible' use of drugs in later adolescence.

Secondly, some participants who had previously used drugs such as amphetamines, LSD, heroin, cocaine or crack-cocaine said they had not done so in the month before the interview. Cassie, for example, was a young offender who had used heroin intravenously for a five-month period when she was fifteen and had become addicted. She was seventeen when we met and had not used heroin for the previous eighteen months. After she had accidentally overdosed she had her stomach pumped and was 'very ill'. She then realised that:

> *It was like, after I started to come off it, it was, I worked out that not only did I have the problems I'd started off with, but I had more problems while I was taking the heroin and speed and that.*

Sam, a fifteen-year-old who had offended and been excluded from school, had started smoking cannabis when he was thirteen and had gone on to use amphetamines, LSD and ecstasy. In the month prior to the interview, however, he said he had only used cannabis. He was asked why he had stopped using these other drugs and said:

> It's 'cos, like, to do with my mum and dad and that. They didn't give me a lot of trust and that, but now they've started to give me trust. That's why I stopped doing the things they asked to stop me, asked me to stop doing. I said 'yeah'...And then after, they started to give me trust and that and they asked me to stop doing them, I said 'alright then', but they started to drink a lot, my mum and dad, so I told them to stop drinking. Once they stopped drinking, I stopped doing drugs.

John had been using crack-cocaine on a regular basis for about two years, but said he had not used any in the two months before the interview. When asked why he had stopped he explained:

> Well, one of my friends went into prison when I was in the bail hostel and I was still taking it, umm, just before he went into prison. Well, I wasn't taking it, he went to prison and I wasn't taking it, I was stopped. He went to prison and I started taking it again and when he came out I stopped, 'cos like, he's proper against it if ya know what I mean. He would have battered me if I'd carried on.

Michael, Cassie, Sam and John demonstrate that 'negotiation of drug use and non-use is an ongoing process throughout the teens' (Measham *et al.*, 1998: p. 10). Their experiences suggest that when vulnerable young people *do* develop drug misuse problems they are often able to modify their use if given appropriate support from families, carers, or friends. John's case in particular demonstrates that if peer groups are an important influencing factor in a young person's decision to take drugs, they may be equally important in their decision to stop using them.

Thirdly, it is important to bear in mind that fluctuations in supplies of drugs in local markets will have a bearing on lifetime prevalence rates and levels of recent use. In addition to this, there may be variations in a young person's ability to afford drugs even if they are available.

Another factor to be considered when thinking about these variations between lifetime prevalence and recent use is that, despite assurances of confidentiality, young people may have worried about incriminating themselves or meeting with disapproval. They may therefore have tended to under-estimate their drug use in the month before the interview. On the other hand, it is possible that as a result of 'macho bravado' some of the young people may have exaggerated the extent of their drug use in the course of their lives (Edmunds *et al.*, 1998).

Previous research has consistently found that 'with increasing age there is an increasing proportion of young people who have used illicit drugs' (ACMD, 1998: p. 18). Such findings were replicated in this study. Everyone in the 19–25 age group had used drugs at some time and this entire group had used cannabis in conjunction with other drugs, or other drugs and volatile substances, compared to approximately two-thirds of the younger age group. A higher proportion of participants in the older age group had used volatile substances than those in the younger age group. This may be a result of changing drug 'fashions'. It is possible that volatile substances may have been more 'fashionable' with young people in the past. On the other hand, it may suggest that young people now have a wider variety of drugs available to them at younger ages and therefore are able to choose to use things other than volatile substances. Comparison of the age groups also shows that in the month before we met, the younger age group had modified its drug taking more than the older age group. This suggests that drug taking behaviour may become more entrenched the longer it goes on.

What Patterns of Drug Use Developed?

In terms of the vulnerable groups, those who had offended, been excluded from school and been looked after in local authority care had modified their drug taking behaviour, more than other groups, in the month before the interview. For example, twelve of the thirteen participants in the offended, excluded and looked after group had *ever* used cannabis, other drugs or volatile substances but just four participants in this group (under a third) said they had used this combination of substances in the month before the interview. Two thirds of this group had therefore changed their patterns of drug use. On the other hand, almost three quarters in the offended and excluded group had *ever* used cannabis, other drugs or volatile substances but this figure had fallen to a third when asked about the drugs they had used in the month before the interview. In this group, therefore, almost half had changed their patterns of drug use.

This demonstrates that the relationship between drug use and 'vulnerability' is extremely complex. Although the former group had the highest lifetime prevalence rates of drug use, they had modified their behaviour in relation to drugs more than those in other groups in the month before the interview. Those who appear to be most at risk of developing drug misuse problems therefore also appear the most able to modify their drug taking behaviour over time.

> Perhaps the more chaotic one's drug use is, the more one is motivated to change it.

In all six people who took part in the study had used drugs intravenously, although they were not necessarily doing so at the time of the interviews. Once again, the intravenous users were fairly evenly distributed across the vulnerable groups rather than being concentrated in the group that had experienced the greatest degree of overlapping disadvantages. For most of the young people, however, intravenous use appeared to represent a significant threshold in drug use over which they were not prepared to step at this point in their drug taking careers. Drug injecting and intravenous users were, on the whole, evaluated negatively. Intravenous use tended to be associated with a loss of control:

Injections bring you right down to the ground.

and with disease:

It's the quickest way to catch a disease.

Others rejected the idea of intravenous use on the grounds that they 'hate needles' and felt it was something they would never consider doing. Others said:

I wouldn't disrespect my body like that.

Or:

It's sick. I couldn't stab myself in the arm just for a buzz. It's sick.

Given the extent of use of drugs such as heroin and cocaine (by sniffing or smoking) amongst these young people it would seem that the stigmas associated with their use might have diminished. On the other hand, it is clear that intravenous use remains largely taboo. What is worrying is that roughly equal proportions of the younger and older age groups had used drugs intravenously. This suggests that drug users may be initiating intravenous use at younger ages which has health and social implications for the young people concerned as well as public health and social implications.

The discussion has demonstrated that:

- these young people had used an extensive range of illicit drugs and that the levels and frequency of use followed complex patterns
- in terms of lifetime prevalence, those with the greatest clustering of difficulties, that is, those who had offended, been excluded from school and looked after had developed the most problematic levels and types of drug use
- this group had the highest lifetime prevalence of poly-drug use, but they had also appeared to modify their drug taking over time more than other groups.

The patterns and levels of drug use identified, present challenges to the various professionals working with vulnerable young people. In practice, the emphasis must be on reducing the potential harm from drug use and making young people aware of the possible risks associated with use of particular drugs in particular ways. They should also be made aware of the likely dangers of combining different types of drugs.

When Did These Young People Start Using Drugs, Alcohol and Volatile Substances?

It is estimated that between a half and a third of all young people have tried an illicit drug by the time they are fifteen (President of the Council, 1998; SCODA, 1997), that 100,000 16–19 year olds have tried opiates and 400,000 16–24 year olds have tried cocaine (National Strategy for Neighbourhood Renewal, 2000).

In this study, half the young people had first used an illicit drug between the ages of 12 and 14, while a quarter had first tried drugs before they were twelve. Three-quarters had therefore tried an illicit drug *before* they were fourteen. This is younger than age of first use found in studies of young people in the general population, which have suggested that, for example, by the age of fifteen, 40 per cent of boys have tried cannabis and 11 per cent have tried LSD and amphetamines (SCODA, 1997). Other studies have found that between 33 per cent and 40 per cent of young people aged 14–15 has used an illicit drug (Parker and Measham 1994 cited in ACMD, 1998). Furthermore, a comparison between the two age cohorts suggests that the age at which young people begin to use drugs is getting younger. On average, those in the 19–25 age band had begun to use drugs at 14.8 years while for those in the 13–18 age band it was 13.1 years.

When compared with the other vulnerable groups, young people who:

- had offended, been excluded from school *and* been looked after and
- those who had been excluded *only*

had, on average, initiated drug use at the youngest ages. This suggests that, directly or indirectly, these experiences may be especially important in providing young people with opportunities to use drugs or are important in informing their decisions about using them. The average age for initiating drug use in these two groups was 12.5 years. It may also be that being out of school, being looked after and being involved in offending effectively removes the intellectual, emotional and social barriers to drug use. On the other hand, it may be that early use of drugs creates situations in which young people are more likely to become involved in behaviour that may lead to their exclusion from school or offending or being looked after.

Three-quarters of these young people had also first used alcohol before they were fourteen. Once again this suggests that a higher proportion were using alcohol at younger ages when compared with studies of young people in the general population. A study of 23,000 schoolchildren in Exeter, for example, found that approximately 26 per cent of boys and 15 per cent of girls aged 10–11 'had consumed an alcoholic drink within the preceding week'. For 14–15 year olds, this figure rose to 61 per cent of boys and 52 per cent of girls (Balding, 1995, cited in ACMD, 1998: p. 17). Other research has suggested that 'most people have their first taste of alcohol around the age of ten' and that by the age of 16 '90 per cent have tasted alcohol' (Hughes *et al.*, 1997).

It was those who had been excluded from school *only* and those who had been excluded and looked after who had, on average, begun to use alcohol at the youngest ages. The average age at which they had begun to use alcohol was 10.3 years and 10 years respectively. Once again, exclusion from school appears to figure as a prominent factor in early initiation into substance use. It may be that a lack of participation in education leads to these young people being unsupervised for long periods at a time, which may create opportunities in which they can begin to use substances without being detected.

Almost half the young people could be described as 'frequent alcohol users', that is, they used alcohol at least once a week. There was, however, a great deal of variation in the frequency with which they drank and in the amount of alcohol consumed on each drinking occasion. Some young people reported that they would drink anything from eight to twelve pints when they were drinking, or that they might share a bottle of vodka with two or three friends at weekends, others reported that they might just have 'a couple' of drinks at weekends. It was clear that the young people did not especially measure the volume of alcohol consumed and, in particular, did not think of it in terms of 'standard units'. Alcohol was perceived as a part of their normal 'leisure/pleasure' landscape (Parker *et al.*, 1998). Only a minority expressed any concerns about their use of alcohol. Those most likely to do so were young men who, on a number of occasions, expressed a concern about their propensity to violence when they had been drinking. They said things such as 'drinking gets me into trouble', or, 'I don't drink spirits because I get violent when I've been drinking them'.

Over three-quarters had started smoking cigarettes before they were fourteen. This again suggests that these vulnerable young people had started smoking at younger ages than young people in the general population. Studies of young people and smoking have suggested that there may be slight regional variations in the age at which young people begin to smoke. A study in Dundee, for example, showed that 52 per cent of 11–16 year olds had ever smoked compared to 57 per cent of this age group in Blackburn (ACMD, 1998).

On average, those who had been excluded from school *and* looked after and those who had been looked after *only* had started smoking at the youngest ages. The average age for initiating smoking in these two groups, at 9.5 years and 10 years respectively was younger than the average for the young people as a whole. The average age for beginning to smoke across the whole group was 11.6 years: younger than the average age for initiating use of drugs, alcohol or volatile substances.

At the time of our meeting, nearly all the young people were regular smokers, that is, they smoked on a daily basis, but once again there was considerable variation in the amounts they smoked. Some said they would smoke under ten cigarettes a day while others said they smoked as many as forty.

In addition to their use of drugs, alcohol and tobacco, just under half the young people had tried or used volatile substances and of these, over three-quarters had done so before they were fourteen. Lifetime prevalence of volatile substance use is in fact much higher across this group of young people than in studies of young people in the general population. These have shown that 13 per cent of 15–16 year olds had ever used volatile substances (Parker *et al.*, 1995 cited in ACMD, 1998) and that one in twenty boys had used a volatile substance by the age of 15 (SCODA, 1997: p. 6). In this study, one in four of this age group had used volatile substances.

Those who had offended, been excluded from school *and* looked after in the care system had begun to use volatile substances at the youngest ages. While the average age for beginning use of these substances amongst all the young people was 12.7 years, those who had offended, been excluded *and* looked after had begun to use them, on average, at 11.8 years. This group also had the highest proportion of young people who had used volatile substances frequently or had sustained their use over a prolonged period of time. This may be because these young people do not have a great deal of money and volatile substances are the cheapest and most immediately available substances (for example, deodorants, hairsprays, lighter fluid).

The ages at which all groups had initiated use of all substances is summarised in Appendix 2.

Conclusion

This section has shown that those who had offended, been excluded from school *and* who had been looked after in local authority care, had begun using drugs and volatile substances at the youngest ages. This may be a result of the clustering of their vulnerabilities or because in these situations drugs are available and young people are provided with opportunities in which to start using them. On the other hand, it was those who had been excluded from school *only* and those who had been excluded from school *and* looked after who had begun to use alcohol and tobacco at the youngest ages. This suggests that those with the most overlapping disadvantages, in terms of offending, being excluded from school and being looked after, were not vulnerable to initiating use of *all* substances at the youngest ages. If they had been, this group would also have started smoking and drinking before other groups. This suggests that the picture is complex and that the relationship between being excluded from school, offending, being looked after or beginning to use drugs is far from straightforward.

> The age at which these young people had started using the various substances discussed here suggests that those involved in their care and education must make sure that they are aware, from very early ages, of the health risks they face.

Young people should be made aware of the potential consequences of using these substances on their own or in conjunction with others. Given that exclusion from school appears to figure prominently in the early initiation of substance use (whether this precedes or follows exclusion) there is an obvious need to avoid exclusion where this is possible. Equally, there is a need to ensure that, when young people are excluded, they receive appropriate education in relation to the use of drugs and other substances. Their 'disaffection' with the education system may make it necessary to use creative and imaginative forms to 'get the message across'.

Chapter 6

Perceptions and Responses: The 'Why Not?' of Drug Use and Service Interventions

Introduction

This chapter explores further:

- the young people's perceptions of their drug taking
- what they said about service interventions that might help them stop using drugs

How Did These Young People Perceive Their Drug Use?

In terms of lifetime prevalence, many of these young people had fairly complex patterns of drug use and a substantial number, from fairly young ages, had used a range of different drugs. However, in a majority of cases, patterns and levels of use had been significantly modified in the months before the interview. The young people in this study seemed to switch between different drugs or combine different drugs depending on the *purpose* for which they were being used and the *context* in which they were being used (q.v. Measham *et al.*, 1998). John, who we met earlier, had been using crack-cocaine on a daily basis at one point in his life. On occasions, he also combined this with heroin. He explained:

> I was taking it [heroin] for the comedown. No, I wasn't doing it often. Not the heroin.

In making decisions about what drugs to use, and how to use them, the young people seemed to perform a type of cost-benefit analysis. This was clearly evidenced in the views they expressed about intravenous drug use and intravenous users. These young people did not think of themselves in the same way as they thought of people who use drugs intravenously, that is, as 'sick' or 'disgusting'. In consuming the drugs they did, the young people appeared to think of themselves as 'normal' or 'ordinary' and the intravenous user was cast as the 'other' of the 'ordinary' drug user. For most, the costs of intravenous use (in terms of self-image, self-identity and risks to their health) appeared to them to be too high in relation to the benefits they might derive from doing it. The rejection of intravenous use was therefore a rational choice. These rational decisions and calculated choices are witnessed in the extracts below. Paul, for example, said:

> P. *Well, I take drugs, I smoke cannabis and, like, I take ecstasy and that, but cocaine and heroin, I think they're nasty drugs.*
> Q. *Why do you think they're nasty?*
> P. *Because they're so addictive [pause]. A lot of my mates had, like, overdoses on heroin, it just overpowers your body. They say they just, all they wanted was that [heroin], and if they don't get it then they'll do whatever they can to get it.*
> Q. *So you've never tried heroin?*
> P. *Nah, I seen too many kids fuck up on it to start taking it.*

These calculations are also witnessed in Sam's account of the drugs he considered it was 'alright' to take and those it was not. He said he had never tried heroin, cocaine or crack:

> S. *I'd never do that.*
> Q. *Why would you never try them?*
> S. *'Cos they're dirty drugs. They can kill ya. Even though all the others can kill ya, them, they're dirty drugs.*
> Q. *What do you mean, I don't; what does it mean that they're 'dirty'?*
> S. *Like when, sometimes they're mixed up, sometimes they're not mixed up but they're just like, horrible. I've seen people when they've been charlieing [sic] and that, and afterwards they've snorted a line and their nose just starts bleeding an' that. And that, oh no, I can't be doing with that.*

Sam also said that he would never consider trying volatile substances because:

> *They can kill you like, straight away. Glue is just for sad people really, 'cos there's no point in sniffing glue. It does your head in, it does your nose in, it does like your nose an' that. I don't see the point in using glue.*

Jane also demonstrates the kinds of calculations young people make when deciding what drugs to take:

> *I smoke puff, I drink alcohol, I love to get drunk, umm, I did speed recently. I smoke cigarettes, I do puff, I do alcohol, I do speed. If pills [ecstasy] were offered to me I'd do them, I would do them. If coke was offered to me I'd do it. Trips, no, speed not so much, because I don't like speed.*

When Jane was asked if she had ever tried using heroin, she said:

> *No, and I never would. I've been offered brown but I would never take it 'cos that's just over the top. I know it's the same sort of, I know it's the same category as cocaine but I would never take it ever 'cos I know how addictive it can be. I just wouldn't go, I wouldn't put myself that low to take it.*

Similarly, Michael told us that he would not take heroin or ecstacy:

> *M. Yeah, cocaine, LSD, but I didn't get an effect off that [laughs] I was unlucky.*
> *Q. You've never tried heroin?*
> *M. Wouldn't touch it, or ecstasy.*
> *Q. Why is that then?*
> *M. 'Cos at the end of the day, if someone wants to take heroin, that's their own, that's their own point...was always scared of heroin as a child because my dad knew someone that used to take heroin...I've sat there and heard him jacking up [laughs]...I don't think a fix is a good thing.*
> *Q. So it put you off, that you were growing up around people who were using it?*
> *M. Mmmm*
> *Q. And it made you frightened of it?*
> *M. Not frightened, it's just, I don't want to touch it. Not frightened but I'm very wary. I'm more wary than frightened.*
> *Q. Do you think you might ever be tempted to try it in the future?*
> *M. I very much doubt it. My girlfriend did it while I was in the secure unit and I absolutely went mad, and, er, no, I'd never take it.*

These extracts show that young people are often put off taking particular drugs as a result of the experiences of peers and people they know. A kind of 'street wisdom' that is sometimes misinformed, (for example, some seemed to think that injecting heroin was 'disgusting' or dangerous but smoking it wasn't) seems to surround these young people's views about using particular drugs in particular ways. Their choice of language is illuminating. 'Dirty drugs' (i.e. drugs that are adulterated) have 'nasty' effects on the user (i.e. turn them into 'addicts') and to want to experience such effects, one has to put oneself 'low' (i.e. have no respect for oneself). These are messages that can be explored and reinforced in drugs prevention education.

Rational calculations were also clearly in evidence when young people weighed up the price of drugs against the benefits that they might expect to derive from their use. Anna, for example, was a fifteen-year-old who had offended and been excluded from school. She had started using cannabis when she was thirteen and at fifteen had started experimenting with cocaine and ecstasy. She had taken cocaine every weekend for a period of about three months and tried ecstasy three times. She was now able, therefore, to compare cocaine and ecstasy and felt that she would rather use ecstasy than cocaine because cocaine was:

...too dear for such a little buzz. It's not worth paying for it.

That young people make rational choices in relation to drug use, and appear to decline use of certain drugs because of what they know about them from their own experience, suggests that, in practice the potential benefits, as well as the potential costs, of using particular drugs need to be explored with them. They might be encouraged to evaluate drugs in terms other than 'the buzz' versus the price, for example, the health costs and opportunity costs of certain drugs. This may be done through education, through creative forms such as drama workshops, or by exposing young people to others who have been through the 'drug experience' and who can talk frankly to them about the benefits and costs of using particular drugs.

About half the young people admitted that they did sometimes worry about their drug use but this did not necessarily stop them from using drugs. Previous research has established that there is in fact considerable ignorance of the risks associated with drug use. A survey of young people conducted by the Health Education Authority in 1995, for example, found that 31 per cent claimed to be unaware of any health risks associated with using ecstasy and 42 per cent did not know of any health risks associated with using LSD (HEA, 1996, cited in McCallum, 1998). Even if they might be aware of long-term risks, young people tend to have 'short-term time perspectives' (McCallum, 1998: p. 28). The risks are therefore always somewhere at some future point that may never be reached. On the other hand, it has been argued 'playing' with risk is part of adolescence and 'growing up' (Parker *et al.*, 1998).

When Jane was asked if she ever worried about her drug use, the risks she was taking appeared to her to be immediate. She said:

> *I worry all the time! Not about puff, but when I take cocaine and speed and E's, I worry all the time, 'cos I think to myself, 'I could die when I take this'. You know what I mean? This could be the last time I ever touch a piece of drug. This could be the last breath I ever take.*

The perceived risks, however, were not enough to stop Jane taking drugs, primarily because she viewed herself as the 'sort of person' who 'likes living life on the edge'.

Paul also said that he had worried about using gas and glue:

> *Well, yeah, I used to worry 'cos, like, I knew this boy, he dropped, he collapsed, like, when we were near him and we were all so wrecked we didn't know nothing about it. And after that I just didn't try it [gas].*

Jamie, a sixteen-year-old, had been using cannabis since he was thirteen. Jamie had offended and been excluded from school. Since he was fifteen he had been regularly using drugs such as amphetamines, cocaine, ecstasy and LSD at weekends. When he was asked if he ever worried about his drug use he said:

> *Yeah, because of smoking bongs* [cannabis pipes] *I worry about getting cancer and when I take the pills and acid, I worry about getting brain damage.*

What Did These Young People Think About Stopping Drugs?

In spite of their expressed concerns, however, only a small proportion of these young people thought they might stop using drugs in the future. This future point, like the place where risks lurk, was a vague and unspecified place that was usually associated with 'settling down' and starting families of their own. In this sense, the aspirations of these young people are very 'mainstream', that is they share the values and aspirations of their less vulnerable peers for jobs, homes and families (Dean and Taylor-Gooby, 1994; Dean and Melrose, 1996; Dean and Melrose, 1999).

When Jane was asked if she thought she would stop using drugs, she said:

> *Probably in the future I'll give it up, 'cos, like, I know for a fact that when I have kids I won't touch any drugs, apart from, like, apart from just smoking cigarettes and drinking alcohol, but even then I'd cut down when I have kids, you know what I mean?*

Similarly, Sam said he might stop in the future:

> *When I settle down and I've got kids, an'* [pause] *'cos the money would have to go on the kids, not on the drugs.*

While their views about stopping drug use might be linked to 'normal' or 'mainstream' aspirations, (for jobs, homes and families) we have seen that these, and many other young people, do not have 'mainstream' opportunities for realising their ambitions and goals. For these vulnerable young people then, stopping drug use might be more difficult than for those young people who have opportunities to work, live independently and establish families of their own (Pearson, 1987, cited in Pitts, 2001).

Although a fair proportion of these young people expressed some concerns about their drug use and approximately a third thought they might stop using drugs in the future, when they were asked specifically if they *wanted* to stop using drugs, only a fifth said they did. Therefore, although many thought they might stop using drugs in the future, very few expressed an *intention* to actually do so. This reveals an underlying tension between their beliefs or attitudes and their behaviour. This is a tension that may potentially be exploited in drugs prevention and awareness education.

Previous research has shown that vulnerable young people, in this case those who were homeless, often exaggerate the extent to which they are in control of their circumstances (Hutson and Liddiard, 1994). Similarly, most of the disadvantaged young people who took part in this study felt that they were in control of their drug use, that they were 'not addicted', that drug use was 'not a problem' and that they could stop using drugs any time they chose. There were no particular differences across the vulnerable groups in relation to this question. Jane, for example, said:

> If I wanted to stop taking them [drugs] I could just stop taking them like that. If I wanted to stop smoking, I could stop like that. It's just a case of wanting to or not, know what I mean? I know that I've got the willpower to stop smoking and stop taking drugs. I've got the willpower, I know I've got the willpower, it's just a case of wanting to use it.

Similarly, Michael said:

> I haven't, there isn't a problem with me smoking puff, I can go a couple of months without smoking puff. I'm not addicted to it. You don't get addicted to puff, you can become dependent on it but I'm stronger than that...I've got the determination to say no.

Billy, a sixteen-year-old who used cannabis regularly and had also tried ecstasy and amphetamine said:

> I could stop if I wanted to but I don't want to.

Indeed, the difference between lifetime prevalence rates and use of drugs in the month before the interview do suggest that many of these young people were able to stop using drugs in problematic ways, often without the intervention of outside agencies. Their views about drug use not being 'a problem' also presents challenges to people working with young people.

> Obviously, young people cannot be forced to accept help if they do not want it and they cannot be made to accept that their drug use is a problem when they clearly do not believe that it is. In these circumstances, it is important to attempt to engender an appreciation of the health risks and opportunity costs, particularly those associated with long term chaotic use.

Of the small group who did talk about what help they thought might be useful for them to stop using drugs, six said they felt support from friends, or from people who have 'been through it' would be useful for them. Paul, for example, said:

> *Really the best thing for people with a drug problem is to be counselled by someone who, like, has had the sort of problem themselves, and, like, beat it themselves. They know exactly what you're going through an', like, they know how hard, how hard it is to stop, instead of like, going to see someone who hasn't got a clue about it and they like put you in one little box. Like, if they done it before, and, like, got off it, and, like, the counselling, then they're the best people to help people 'cos they know exactly what it's like.*

People who became involved in prostitution as juveniles often echoed these sentiments (Melrose *et al.*, 1999). It is clear that young people who live in the social margins do not like being 'preached at' by people who they think 'don't know what they are talking about'. The 'drugs message' needs to be delivered by people whom the young people consider to have 'street cred'. Previous research has established that peer education is valued in the lives of vulnerable young people (Melrose *et al.*, 1999; DoH, 1996; O'Neill *et al.*, 1995). At the same time, however, peers may be a double-edged sword. After all, it was as a result of peer influences and peer networks that many of these young people had become involved in drug taking in the first place and peer influences are also known to be important in the development of offending careers.

Other young people who said they might like help to stop using drugs were unable to articulate the sort of help they thought might be useful. John, for example, thought he might like help to stop using crack, because even though he was managing, at the time of the interview, not to use it, he found the temptation to return to it difficult to resist. He said:

> *I would like help. What sort of help, or what would stop me, well I don't know. Ummm, I would like help.*

Of course, young people may not be aware of what services are available to them and in these circumstances, this would be a difficult question to answer.

Conclusion

This chapter has shown that, although these young people consumed a fairly extensive range of drugs, they did not perceive their drug use to be a 'problem'. Most did not relate their drug use to their vulnerability as offenders, school excludees or young people who had been looked after. Instead, drug use seemed to be regarded as a rather 'normal' activity that they had integrated into their everyday lives. In this sense, their drug taking appears not to be dissimilar to drug taking by their not so vulnerable peers (Parker *et al.*, 1998).

At the same time, however, some underlying contradictions were detected in the views these young people expressed about drugs. For example, at the end of our conversation the young people were asked if they would offer any advice to other young people who might be in similar circumstances to themselves and who might be thinking of beginning to use drugs. Given their confidence in asserting that drugs were 'not a problem' and that they could stop using them if they wanted to, the views elicited in response to this question might seem surprising. Many said they would tell other young people that 'it isn't worth it', that drugs 'muck you up', 'fuck you up' or in other ways 'ruin your life'. On the other hand, a few participants said they would merely offer advice about how to use drugs 'safely'. These contradictory views can be explored and reinforced in drugs prevention education.

> Getting the message across to such young people is likely to be an arduous task.

Chapter 7

Vulnerable Girls and Drugs: Gender Differences in Drug Consumption

Introduction

This chapter is concerned with variations *between* the men and women in this group of vulnerable young people, in patterns of use of:

- drugs
- alcohol
- tobacco
- and volatile substances

In examining these variations, the chapter pays attention to the vulnerability of these young people as:

- young offenders
- young people who have been excluded from school
- young people who have been looked after

in relation to wider, and more enduring, structural factors such as:

- gender inequality
- differences in backgrounds and family situation

When focusing on gender in this discussion it is important to recognise that it is the junction at which inequalities of class, gender and ethnicity collide that determine the experiences of *all* young people. Given the small numbers of young people from ethnic minority groups who took part, however, and the limitations of space, the debate is confined to that of gender differences. It was notable, however, that amongst those who took part in this study, it was those who came from 'mixed parentage' households (African-Caribbean and white British, Pakistani and white British, Maltese and white British) who appeared to have the most problematic levels and patterns of drug use.

Gender and Drug Use

Historically, drug literature has tended to ignore, or not even notice, women's drug use. In recent years, however, a growing body of work has begun to explore this issue in its own right. It has been suggested that as a result of contemporary youth/rave culture, masculinity and femininity have undergone a process of change, which, in conjunction with wider social and economic change, has had deep implications for the experience of both men and women (Henderson, 1999). In particular it has been suggested that the contemporary youth/rave culture has created relationships between boys and girls, young men and young women that are more equal than they have previously been (Merchant and MacDonald, 1994). It may be as a result of this, that generally, young women's drug use appears to be catching up with that of men (Henderson, 1999; McCallum, 1998; Parker *et al.*, 1998). What were once thought to be 'distinctive differences' in patterns of drug use between young men and women, are, in contemporary youth drug culture, 'disappearing' (Parker *et al.*, 1998: p. 14) and 'an increasing proportion of hard drug misusers are women' (Social Services Committee 1985: p. iv, cited in Oppenheimer, 1989: p. 178). In the eleven-year period from 1975–86, for example, there was a six-fold increase in the numbers of women, under the age of twenty-five, notified to the Home Office as opiate users (Home Office, 1987, cited in Oppenheimer, 1989: p. 183).

Below, the experiences of the young women are explored. They show that amongst disadvantaged and vulnerable young people, gender differences in drug use patterns appear to have reversed and that many hard drug users are women. First, what these young women said about their motivations for using drugs is examined.

What Did the Young Women Say About Their Motivations for Using Drugs

The young men and women being looked at here had, in the main, begun to use drugs for different reasons. Approximately a quarter of the young women said they had started using drugs to escape from other problems in their lives, that is, were 'oblivion seekers'.

'Rachel'

Rachel, an 18-year-old who had started drinking heavily at the age of 12 after her mother had died, was excluded from school when she was fifteen for 'bad behaviour'. She committed an alcohol-related offence, for which she was convicted, when she was sixteen. She was asked about her background, where she went to school, how she got on at school 'and things like that'. She said:

Oh well, when I was eleven, my mum passed away, and that's when, when I was about twelve, I started drinking 'cos of the death of my mum.

'Debbie'

Debbie, a sixteen-year-old who had been excluded from school and looked after said that 'in hindsight' she had begun to use drugs:

...to block things out, but I didn't think that at the time.

Debbie, who was living in a hostel at the time of the interview, had used a mind-boggling mixture of drugs in the past, including crack, heroin, and methadone. She had taken heroin in the month before the interview but said she was not regularly using any drugs.

Another quarter of the women said they had started using drugs because they wanted to escape from other problems *and* because they wanted to 'fit in' with drug using peers or a drug-using environment. These were 'oblivion *and* acceptance seekers'. Beth, from whom we heard earlier, and Josie, whose story we hear below, provide typical examples of the young women who said they had begun to use drugs for a combination of these reasons.

'Josie'

Josie said she was looked after by the local authority when she was nine because:

...my mum couldn't cope financially and her boyfriend had been beating me up.

She had been convicted of 'common assault' when she was thirteen. She stopped attending school when she was fourteen and living in a foster placement. At around this time she was using drugs such as cannabis, volatile substances and 'base' (amphetamine), having first tried cannabis and gas when she was thirteen. She was fifteen when we met and had tried crack three times. She said she used drugs because:

Drugs make you happy and I'm not very happy. I carried on using base because it cheers you up and makes you feel good about yourself.

She had used volatile substances because 'everyone else was'.

Women constituted the majority of the 'oblivion seekers' and 'oblivion and acceptance seekers' identified in the study. Under half the men said they had initiated drug use in order to escape from other problems with which they were confronted. Other recent work in this field has also shown that men and women begin to use drugs for different reasons. Women often begin to use drugs 'to cope with very real pressures and the underlying tensions of their lives' while men use them 'to deal with external pressures and to feel disinhibited' (McCallum, 1998: p. 10; q.v. Ettorre, 1992; Breeze, 1985).

On the whole, although six of the women could be classified as 'thrill and acceptance' seekers, their motivations for beginning to use drugs were slightly less varied than the young men. Generally, the young women drew most frequently on a discourse of 'acceptance by others' when explaining their reasons for initiating drug use. This was mentioned by no less than two-thirds of the women, although it was not necessarily the dominant theme in the accounts of all of these.

When the differences in the backgrounds of these young women and men are examined, we can begin to understand the 'very real pressures and underlying tensions' with which many of the young women were attempting to cope. Their desire for 'escape', or 'oblivion', becomes understandable when their behaviour is located within the context of their whole lives. Likewise, it is possible to understand why many of these young women might have been keen to gain acceptance in peer group networks.

The following section explores these young women's status as:

- young offenders
- young people who had been excluded from school
- young people who had been looked after
- their family relations and the backgrounds from which they had come

before examining differences in patterns of consumption of substances and considering what this suggests about the relationship between gender, vulnerability and drug use.

What Made the Young Women Vulnerable?

The young women were predominately concentrated in two of the vulnerable groups identified in the research. Over half (nine) were concentrated in the offended *and* excluded group, representing more than a third of this whole group. Another quarter (four) were concentrated in the offended, excluded *and* looked after group, again representing approximately a third of the whole group. One woman had offended *only* and one had been looked after *only*. No women had been excluded from school *only* and no women had offended *and* been looked after.

Approximately half the women had already started using illicit substances *before* they became involved in offending, were excluded from school or were looked after. This suggests that many of the young women became vulnerable to drug use as a result of things *other* than offending, exclusion from school or being looked after in the local authority care system.

Backgrounds and Family Circumstances of the Young People

Although many of these young people came from unstable family situations, on the whole it was the young women who most often came from disorganised families. None came from nuclear families and half had come from reconstituted families where they had experienced step-parenting. As we already know, disrupted family relationships are correlated with many other types of problematic behaviour in adolescence (OFSTED, 1996; Lloyd *et al.*, 1998; Martin *et al.*, 1999; Melrose *et al.*, 1999). Additionally, when a new partner is introduced into a household after parental divorce, adolescent girls tend to have more difficulties adjusting to the situation than boys (Lloyd *et al.*, 1998).

Over a quarter of the young women said they had been sexually abused when they were young compared to just one man. It may be that a young man might be less likely than a young woman to 'disclose' this sort of information in an interview situation when the interview was 'about drugs' or when talking to a female interviewer.

Those working in the field of child abuse recognise that incidents of child sexual abuse are under-reported (Wyatt *et al.*, 1993). There are indications that, in populations of drug addicted and alcoholic women, the incidence of child sexual abuse is extremely high. One study has estimated that between 70 per cent and 80 per cent of women with serious drinking problems 'are victims of some form of sexual abuse' (McCallum, 1998: p. 31). Given this under-reporting, we can assume that the incidence is higher for *both* the young women *and* the young men.

The young women also reported more frequently than the young men that they had experienced conflict in their family relationships. This may be because there are higher levels of *actual conflict* in their families (and the incidence of sexual abuse reported here would suggest that there is) rather than, as has previously been suggested, because male and female 'heroin addicts' 'perceive' family interactions differently (Binion, 1979, cited in Oppenheimer, 1989: p. 186). This is not to suggest that 'gender' and 'perception' are unconnected but to argue that it is possible that women report negative childhood experiences more often than men because they actually *have* more negative childhood experiences. Their negative perceptions may actually have a material basis!

In addition to their experiences of unstable family backgrounds, sexual abuse and conflict in their families, more of the young women reported that their parents used drugs. This has previously been identified as one of a range of factors that is thought to put young people at greater risk of developing problematic patterns of drug use themselves (HAS, 1996).

Gender Differences in Patterns of Consumption of Drugs, Alcohol, Tobacco and Volatile Substances

In terms of the drugs they had *ever* used, almost three-quarters of the women had used cannabis in combination with other drugs or volatile substances compared to approximately half the men. Whereas a quarter of men had only *ever* used cannabis, no women had done so. Almost two-thirds of the women had used amphetamines, just over half had used cocaine, just over a third had used heroin and ecstasy, a third had used crack-cocaine and a fifth had used LSD. With the use of these 'other' drugs, more men had used crack, LSD and ecstasy and equal numbers of men and women had used cocaine and amphetamines. With heroin, though, it was a different story. Of the ten people who had used this drug, six were women; that is, almost half the women we spoke to compared to just over one tenth of the men. Intravenous use was also more prevalent amongst the women than amongst the men. A quarter had used drugs intravenously compared to just one twentieth of the men. Unsurprisingly, the women also reported experiencing withdrawal symptoms more often than the young men.

The trend for women increasingly to consume hard drugs has been confirmed in previous research and the finding of higher levels of opiate and intravenous use among these young women correlates with findings from an Australian study of young people in custody. It found 'higher levels of heroin use and HIV risk taking behaviour' among the young women (McCallum, 1998: pp. 14–15). In the USA, opiate use has been increasing more rapidly amongst women than amongst men (Ettorre, 1992: p. 73). In the nineteenth century, however, women opiate users were thought to outnumber men by three to one, in both Britain and the USA, therefore, the apparent propensity for men more frequently to be heroin addicts may be a phenomenon peculiar to the twentieth century. On the other hand, it may be that women's use of this substance has remained relatively invisible until now or that it has increased quite drastically among young women who are rendered vulnerable as a result of 'negative stresses' in their lives.

Previous research has suggested that 'in response to stress, girls tend to self-destruct with quietly disturbed behaviours rather than 'act out' as boys do' (Shultz, 1990 cited in Turner *et al.*, 1995: p. 30, cited in McCallum, 1998: p. 25). This tendency seems to be witnessed in many of the young women's motivations for using drugs (desire for oblivion, acceptance), in the drugs they use, and the way them use them (heroin and intravenous use). Given the less stable, and more abusive, family situation from which the young women have come, and other life stresses they have experienced, for example, offending, being excluded from school and being looked after, their desire for 'oblivion' seems quite understandable. Given also their backgrounds and experiences it might not surprise us to learn that the women who took part in this study had actually outdone their male peers when it came to consumption of illicit substances.

As well as higher lifetime prevalence, and more problematic patterns of drug use amongst the women, the women had appeared to modify their drug taking behaviour in the month before the interview *less* than the young men. In the month before the interview, *over half* the women had used cannabis, other drugs *and* volatile substances compared to *less than one fifth* of the men. Over a quarter of the men said they had not used any drugs in the month before the interview but under a tenth of women gave this reply. Women's patterns of drug use in the month before the interview suggest that their drug use had become more entrenched than the men's. There is also the possibility that because of the gender dynamics in the interview situation (female to female interviews) that women were more honest about their drug use in the past month, or alternatively, that they felt the need to exaggerate their drug taking across their lifetime and in the past month. The researchers did not detect blatant exaggeration, however. In particular, women's continued use of volatile substances suggests that they take longer to 'grow out of' this form of substance use than the young men *or* that they have less money and access to other drugs *or* that volatile substances are more available to them (e.g. hairsprays, deodorants etc.). The differences in patterns of drug and volatile substance use cannot be attributed to age because the average age of men and women in the sample is very similar: 16.7 years for the former and 16.5 years for the latter.

Not only was lifetime prevalence, use in the past month and intravenous use higher amongst the women, but overall, they had tended to initiate drug use at younger ages than the men. Over a third had started using drugs before they were twelve compared to a fifth of the men.

Examining these differences in patterns of drug use suggests that vulnerable young women are at greater risk of beginning to use illicit substances at younger ages than their male peers. Further, because of the particular drugs and combinations of drugs they were using, the young women were more likely to go on to develop types and levels of drug use that are potentially damaging to the young women themselves as well as to society.

Recent research that has looked at women's alcohol use has also suggested that women's consumption levels are beginning to 'catch up' with those of men and that young women are increasingly indulging in 'heavy episodic drinking' (McCallum, 1998: p. 14; q.v. Ettorre, 1992; Breeze, 1985). The women in this study had, on average, started drinking before the men. A third had started using alcohol before they were twelve compared to a fifth of the men. At the time of the interviews, half the women could be described as 'frequent drinkers', that is, they would drink at least once a week. Given that the majority of these young people were under eighteen, this suggests a worrying trend.

The women had also started smoking before the men. Two thirds had started smoking before they were twelve compared to half the men and, when we met, a higher proportion of women were regular smokers. A number of studies have indicated that the prevalence of smoking is higher amongst young women than young men and have noted that young women tend to smoke more than young men (Lloyd *et al.*, 1998; McCallum, 1998). These studies have also noted that young women are beginning to smoke at much younger ages than they did in the past (McCallum, 1998: p. 13). It has been suggested that for young women, smoking represents a 'potent symbol of power and independence' and is associated with 'the construction of an adult female social identity' (McCallum, 1998: p. 17; q.v. Graham, 1987, cited in Ettorre, 1992).

In addition to higher levels of drug, alcohol and tobacco consumption, volatile substance use was more prevalent amongst these women than amongst the men. Two thirds of women had used volatile substances compared to less than a quarter of the men. In this instance, however, men had tended to start using volatile substances before the women but, as we have seen, fewer men than women had taken these substances in the month before the interview. That women 'surpass their male equivalents when it comes to sniffing solvents' has been found in other studies of young people in the general population (Parker *et al.* 1995, cited in Henderson, 1999: p. 36).

> The young women who took part in this study had surpassed their male equivalents in every sphere of intoxication and the patterns and levels of their drug use would lead us to conclude that they are more vulnerable than their equally vulnerable male peers to developing drug misuse problems.

This suggests that these young women are responding to their difficulties and situations in typically gendered ways. That is, they were 'trying to cope with very real pressures' (McCallum, 1998) with 'quietly disturbed behaviours' rather than 'acting out' 'as boys do' (Schultz, 1990, cited in McCallum, 1990).

These differences in patterns of consumption in both licit and illicit substances have two sets of implications. The first are social and result from different gender role expectations. These are discussed below. The second are physical and result from biological sex differences. As a result of these differences, women 'reach the same blood alcohol level as men with lesser amounts of alcohol consumed' (McCallum, 1998: p. 7; Breeze, 1985: p. 2). It has also been argued that biological differences affect the metabolism of drugs such as cannabis in the body. The greater amount of fat tissue in female bodies is thought to affect the way in which the female body metabolises THC (the active ingredient in cannabis). The fat tissue stores and gradually releases THC and it therefore stays in the female body longer with the result that 'female cannabis use and effects fluctuate more than males' (McCallum, 1998). There is also evidence of differences in the way male and female bodies metabolise nicotine and other drugs that are fat soluble (McCallum, 1998). On the whole, young women appear to be unaware of the sex-specific harm that may result from drug use and it has been argued that this general lack of awareness 'highlights the deficits in their knowledge' (McCallum, 1998: p. 8).

Why is Gender Important in Interpreting the Evidence?

Given the prevailing gender hierarchy and gender role expectations that result from it, it is obvious that different social meanings will attach to the use of different substances depending on whether the user is male or female. Whereas for men, drinking and even drunkenness may represent a 'rite of passage' to adulthood and masculinity, the same is not true for women. Women's drunkenness has historically met with disapproval (McCallum, 1998; Ettorre, 1992). Additionally, in the past, female drug users were condemned more severely than their male counterparts (Henderson, 1999; McCallum, 1998; Oppenheimer, 1989). Within drug cultures, women's drug use has tended to be more stigmatised than that of men's, and women's use of alcohol and drugs has tended to be associated with sexual promiscuity. Women's drug use has, in the past, been interpreted as a form of 'double deviance', that is, as a deviation from 'normative' behaviour as well as a deviation from expected female gender role behaviour (Henderson, 1999; McCallum, 1998; Ettorre, 1992).

If male and female role expectations are different, it is hardly surprising that young men and women may seek to acquire quite different sorts of 'reputations'.

It has been suggested, for example, that while young women may seek to establish a 'conforming' reputation, young men may seek to do the opposite (McCallum, 1998). For young men, therefore, gaining a reputation as a 'trouble-maker' at school, or as an 'offender', or even as a 'drug taker', may represent an 'accolade' providing a route to status enhancement within particular peer groups. On the other hand, when a young woman engages in the same behaviour it may be interpreted as a *loss* of reputation through which her identity is 'spoiled' (Ettorre, 1992) and which positions her in a cycle of 'shame' (McCallum, 1998). The shame itself may come to function as an 'invisible prison' (Rosenbaum, 1981 cited in Oppenheimer, 1989) in which both her 'bad' behaviour and her drug taking may escalate.

Alternatively, it has been suggested recently that, as a result of wider social and cultural changes, women have been able to 'reclaim the right to pleasure' and as a consequence, are increasingly likely to rebel against the idea that they must be 'good girls' (McCallum, 1998). In this context women's drug use may represent a form of 'rebellion' for many young women who find that the female stereotype of 'the wholesome good girl just isn't a turn on' (Banwell and Young, 1993, cited in McCallum, 1998: p. 10). Because, when they are approaching adulthood, young women have fewer opportunities than young men, a woman may perceive drug use as a way of 'broadening her horizons' and 'accomplishing independence' (Oppenheimer, 1989). If she becomes addicted, however, all that remains available for her is a 'career of narrowing options', that is, through addiction a woman's life options are gradually 'funnelled' (Rosenbaum, 1981: p. 11, cited in Oppenheimer, 1989: p. 184).

It has also been argued recently that drugs such as amphetamine, LSD and ecstasy may represent for women a means of staying in control (of their sexuality), claiming pleasure and still conforming to the stereotypical female role (McCallum, 1998). It is argued that these drugs are not associated with promiscuity in the way that women's drunkenness or heroin and cocaine use, have traditionally been (McCallum, 1998; Merchant and MacDonald, 1994; Ettorre, 1992). Reclaiming the 'right to pleasure' through indulging in activities that have traditionally been regarded as 'male preserves', however, is a double edged sword for women as there is a lack of 'social benchmarks' against which they may gauge their consumption of alcohol and other licit or illicit substances. In the absence of such benchmarks, women may tend to adopt 'male' norms in relation to the consumption of alcohol and other substances (McCallum, 1998). Doing so, however, potentially has greater health and social costs for women than for men.

Conclusion

This discussion has shown that 'gender' is an important tool in explaining women's use of drugs and other substances as well as social reactions to it. It has been suggested that using drugs may represent a means by which women are able to escape the narrow confines of gender role expectations. On the other hand, drug use may represent conformity to those same expectations by 'blocking out' problems and 'coping' or by using drugs that allow young women to 'stay in control'. Drug use may also represent a means of rebelling against gender role expectations.

> For the young women in this study, drug use seemed to represent a typically gendered way of approaching their problems. They had 'kept quiet' about their problems and sought solutions to them in self-destructive ways. In so doing, they had turned their problems in on themselves rather than seeking solutions to them by challenging their social basis. Equally, their desire for 'acceptance' betrayed highly gendered motivations to be approved of and liked.

This study certainly seem to confirm that there is 'something going on' in relation to gender and drug use, particularly amongst women who are disadvantaged in terms of both the prevailing class and gender hierarchy. It may be that these findings are purely an artefact of the groups on whom the research was focused, and that, because these women were already involved in other forms of problematic behaviour, it is to be expected that their drug use would be more problematic than young women's who are not so vulnerable. On the other hand, these findings may reflect trends reported in other recent research (Parker *et al.*, 1998; Measham *et al.*, 1998; McCallum, 1998). Whether a result of sample selection or a reflection of what is happening in the real world, these findings present specific challenges to those involved in working with young women and vulnerable young women in particular.

> Certainly, the experiences of the young women in the sample group show that amongst disadvantaged and vulnerable young people, gender differences in drug use patterns appear to have reversed and that many hard drug users are women.

There is an obvious need to educate young women about the sex-specific harm that may result from the use of drugs and other substances. There is also a need to equip young women to cope with problems they may have encountered in their lives and to make them aware of their social basis. Through doing so, young women may be encouraged to understand their disadvantage and vulnerability as the result of social and economic arrangements rather than as the pathological symptoms of individual failure.

To develop appropriate responses to young women who become involved in problematic drug use we need to know more about the gender specific effects of, and gender specific meanings that attach to, experiences of offending, being excluded from school, being looked after and indeed, drug use. Unfortunately, our knowledge in this sphere is sadly underdeveloped and this remains a question for future research.

Chapter 8

Conclusions: Responding to Vulnerable Young People and Drug Use

Introduction

Concerns about the use of drugs, alcohol and tobacco have been with us throughout the twentieth century and before. However, as we enter the new millennium, these concerns have focused on the use of drugs by vulnerable young people. This results, in part, from the recognition that the conditions in which vulnerable young people make the transition to adulthood may make it more likely that they will begin to use drugs.

This study has provided further evidence that vulnerable young people experience a range of intersecting problems and difficulties:

- poverty
- disorganised families
- the spatial concentration of economic and social disadvantage
- and the young people's overlapping experiences of:
  - offending
  - being excluded from school
  - being looked after in the local authority care system

The young people had:

- used an extensive range of drugs
- from a young age
- and for a variety of reasons.

There are also some indications that vulnerable young women appear to be more at risk of developing drug problems than their equally vulnerable male peers.

Vulnerability

We have seen that previous research has suggested that some young people are more vulnerable than others to developing drug misuse problems because their experiences of:

- offending
- being excluded from school
- being looked after in the local authority care system

are thought to put them more at risk of doing so (HAS, 1996). In fact the evidence from *this* study suggests that the issues are considerably more complex and that other issues such as gender must also be taken into account. Overall, it would appear that it is other influences and factors in the young person's experience and environment that render them vulnerable to drug misuse problems. In the development of problematic levels and patterns of drug use, it is:

- material deprivation
- family and community poverty and disorganisation
- experiences of abuse and neglect

in conjunction with being:

- male or female
- black or white

that are as important as experiences of offending, exclusion from school or being looked after in themselves. The fact that drug use is taking place within a social and cultural context where taking drugs is increasingly accepted as an aspect of mainstream leisure activities, is also important.

There are still, however, differences between social groups in the way in which 'problematic' behaviour is constructed and perceived. For example, does an Eton schoolboy who truants, or who, as a result of 'high spirits' is convicted of a breach of the peace, or causing an affray *automatically* become vulnerable to developing drug misuse problems? The answer is 'of course not'.

> This study has shown that the young people who took part often faced extreme and multiple difficulties in their lives and their chances of developing problems in relation to drug use are increased as a result of these.

Vulnerability to drug use and to developing drug misuse problems, as this book has shown, derives from the interaction of a whole host of factors. Amongst these are:

- mixing with drug using peers
- coming from communities where there is a spatial concentration of social disadvantage and where drug taking is 'normal'
- disorganised family backgrounds and
- unhappy experiences in families and schools

The government's ten-year drug strategy acknowledges that there are links between social deprivation and problematic drug use (President of the Council, 1998). Acknowledging this link is important, especially as it had been resisted by the previous administration (Pearson, 1999). Government policies have so far done little to tackle inequality (Elliot *et al.*, 2000) and therefore, success in tackling drug use amongst young people who are vulnerable or disadvantaged may be limited.

Young people who are:

- excluded from school
- involved in offending behaviour or
- looked after in the local authority care system

are increasingly described as 'socially excluded'. Although this term is subject to considerable debate and disagreement, it has served an important function as a unifying concept for a range of government initiatives that have been introduced. Below, the meaning of social exclusion is examined and recent policy developments, such as educational initiatives, 'Quality Protects', developments in the juvenile justice system, 'Connections' and the 'New Deal' are explored. These have been introduced to combat 'a combination of linked problems such as unemployment, poor skills, low income, poor housing and high crime environments' (National Strategy for Neighbourhood Renewal, 2000) that is, the Government's official definition of 'social exclusion'. It is important to note that it is difficult to comment on the efficacy of these developments because they are all relatively recent and it is not always clear what the practical implications of them might be. After examining these initiatives, the implications of the findings reported here are discussed in terms of their implications for practitioners working in different practice situations.

Inequality and Deprivation

We saw in Chapter 2 that as a result of social and economic change over the past twenty-five years, levels of inequality in Britain have increased enormously and continue to do so (Coyle and Grice, 2000; Elliot *et al.*, 2000). It is young people who have been the casualties of these changes as they have been expelled from the labour market and their social rights have been undermined. Many young people are now described as 'socially excluded' and although we are talking about the same young people what we mean when we say they are 'socially excluded' varies depending on our political or philosophical viewpoint.

On one hand, 'social exclusion' is understood as a consequence of poverty in that it results from people's inability to participate in the 'customary life of society'. When the resources of an individual, a family or a group 'are so seriously below those commanded by an average individual or family' they are 'excluded from ordinary living patterns, customs and activities' (Townsend, 1979: p. 32, cited in Levitas, 1999: p. 12). In other formulations, and particularly in the way that 'social exclusion' is defined in the discourse of the New Labour government, 'the key element is labour force attachment' (Levitas, 1999: p. 12). In this discourse, 'paid work is represented as the primary or sole legitimate means of integrating individuals of working age into society' (Levitas, 1999: p. 12). In the formulation of the New Right, a third approach to social exclusion is suggested. This emphasises the cultural and moral roots of poverty and focuses on the 'threat' to the social order posed by workless households, young men who are unemployed and criminally inclined, and never married, young single parent mothers (Murray 1990, 1999 cited in Levitas, 1999).

When socially excluded young people are being discussed, therefore, sometimes what is being referred to is young people who lack the resources to follow the kinds of lifestyles and living patterns that many people take for granted, sometimes it is young people who are not attached to the labour market, and sometimes it is young people who are morally deficient, unemployed, criminally inclined and sexually promiscuous (Levitas, 1999). The point is, however their social exclusion is explained, the many difficulties and problems they face do not disappear.

Reducing School Exclusion

Given that the New Labour government views social exclusion as a result of lack of labour market attachment, a great deal of importance has been attached to developing educational and training opportunities. Educational attainment and qualifications are an important prerequisite to ensuring entry to the labour market. It is no accident, therefore that the first report of the Social Exclusion Unit (SEU) focused on young people who were not participating in education—either as a result of exclusion or truancy. The number of exclusions steadily increased throughout the 1990s and reached a peak of 12,700 in 1996–97 (Department for Education and Employment, 1998). Truancy, however, is an even more widespread problem than school exclusions. After having reviewed the evidence in relation to these issues, the SEU report (1998) established a new exclusion strategy. Central to this is the aim of reducing the number of permanent exclusions by one third by 2002 (Department for Education and Employment, 1999). Schools have also been provided with resources to assist in the prevention of exclusion and there is a requirement that by 2002 all Local Education Authorities provide appropriate, full time, education for all young people excluded for more than three weeks. Similar targets have been set in relation to truancy. Additionally the amount of time lost as a result of truancy should be reduced by a third by 2002. Schools are required to set their own targets in relation to this and the courts have been given additional powers to ensure a young person's attendance at school.

The government's approach to addressing the social exclusion that may result from non-participation in education, however, is more wide-ranging than merely focusing on those who are not attending or who are excluded from school. Prevention via early intervention, for example through the 'Sure Start' initiative, and an emphasis on literacy and numeracy have also been central. In respect to literacy and numeracy, schools are required to work towards set targets; and practices introduced under the Conservative administration, such as the publication of school 'league tables', and a powerful inspection regime under OFSTED, have continued to have a high profile. Inspection teams have been sent in to rescue schools or local education authorities where they are deemed to have repeatedly 'failed' to meet the targets set.

These initiatives have often met with controversy and in some cases considerable resistance. The fact remains, however, that schools are required to respond to the needs of these vulnerable young people in a context where they are required to compete for pupils and where some schools appear to be admitting a disproportionately high number of young people with emotional, social and educational difficulties (Gewisty *et al.*, 1995). Teacher's unions have complained that the emphasis on reducing school exclusions, which fell to 10,400 in 1998–99, has meant that schools are being asked to tolerate unacceptable levels of disruptive behaviour. It is a difficult task to balance the needs of a small disruptive minority within the wider school community and this issue may never be satisfactorily resolved. It is likely that there will always be a small group of pupils who will require education outside of the mainstream classroom but what has not been acceptable is the lack of alternative provision for these young people and their families. How far the Government has achieved its target of providing appropriate full-time education for those out of school is at present unclear. It is encouraging, however, that the plight of those who, for whatever reason, are not receiving an education, and who will consequently be disadvantaged in later life, has been recognised and that additional resources are being invested in this area.

These changes have a number of potential effects on the experiences of the most vulnerable young people. Continued participation in education, while not necessarily reducing exposure to drugs, can introduce a number of protective factors such as access to personal, health and social education. However, the amount and nature of drugs education made available by schools will continue to be important, and it may be more appropriate for these to be offered in collaboration with other agencies, such as the youth service.

'Quality Protects'

Young people who are looked after provide a good example of those who have often not received appropriate education and who are therefore disadvantaged in later life. The education of young people in the public care system has long been neglected, despite evidence demonstrating the poor educational outcomes experienced by this group. More generally, the 'life chances' of children looked after by local authorities have been identified as poorer than those of their peers (Department of Health, 1998a). Young people in the public care system have been identified as one of the groups who are particularly at risk of social exclusion. While it is recognised that negative family experiences are essential to understanding the difficulties experienced by young people looked after, it has been increasingly recognised that the care system itself has done little to help. On the publication of Sir William Utting's Review of the Safeguards for Children Living Away from Home (1997), Secretary of State for Health, Frank Dobson, commented that the report revealed 'the failure of the whole system' to provide a 'secure and decent childhood for some of the most vulnerable children'. Although these comments have been echoed in similar statements over recent decades, it is probably true to say that the government programme subsequently initiated is one of the most ambitious to date.

Central to the government's response has been the 'Quality Protects' initiative (Department of Health, 1998b). This is a major three-year programme that aims to improve services for young people who are looked after and which is backed by a £375 million grant over the three years. Six priority areas have been identified for improvement, namely increasing the range of adoptive, foster and residential placements for young people who are looked after, improving after-care services, enhancing management information systems, improving assessment, care planning and record keeping, strengthening quality assurance systems and consultation with young people. A series of eight key objectives, each with a set of linked sub-objectives, is central to the programme. Of particular relevance to the young people interviewed as part of this study is the objective that young people who are in need and young people who are looked after should gain maximum advantage from educational opportunities, health and social care. This is to be achieved by improving educational attainment, reducing the rate of offending and supporting black and ethnic minority children. Local Authorities are required to set their own objectives in respect of each of these targets and are required to review their progress annually.

To support the implementation of this programme, consultative guidance has been issued relating to the education and health of young people who are looked after (Department for Education and Employment/Department of Health, 1999). This gives greater attention to the processes through which professionals can provide support in these areas. Thus, in relation to health, the proposed guidance strengthens arrangements for medical assessments, requires better co-ordination and transfer of medical records and the development of health care plans where these are appropriate. New National Standards have also been set for foster care (National Foster Care Association, 1999) and a framework for the full assessment of children in need developed. A *Leaving Care Bill* is also before Parliament; this includes proposals to provide further support to young people leaving the care system in respect of accommodation, education and training. These proposals would obviously have a beneficial effect for the young people who took part in this study. If they are to be successful, however, it is essential that the improved gathering of baseline information, planning and assessment takes place in an integrated way across different agencies, thus ensuring that the multiple needs of young people looked after are appropriately addressed.

'Connections'

Another important development that potentially has implications for the sorts of young people who took part in this study is the 'Connections' initiative. Recognising the need for 'more consistent coverage and provision for the youth service' and 'the importance of high quality careers advice' the Connections initiative promises 'a universal youth support service'. It aims to provide 'personal advice and support to all young people and will work closely with other specialist services' (National Strategy for Neighbourhood Renewal, 2000). The Connections service 'represents a huge opportunity to improve the quality and co-ordination of support for young people'. However, there is a need to ensure that the new service 'meshes effectively' with other existing services within the local area and that the specialist services to which young people may be referred 'are available and suitable' (National Strategy for Neighbourhood Renewal, 2000).

'Persistent, nasty little juveniles'

'Persistent, nasty little juveniles' is a comment attributable to former Home Secretary, Kenneth Clarke, which he made in the context of attacking the social work profession for 'not succeeding with children' (Clarke, 1993, cited in Garrett, 1999: p. 294). The discourse that has demonised young people as a 'threat to communities' did not originate with New Labour, who have merely inherited and uncritically accepted this paradigm from the previous administration.

Since New Labour came to power, young people who are involved in particular forms of disorder have been subject to various 'innovations' in the youth justice system which is currently 'awash with experimental programmes and trials' (Muncie, 1999: p. 148).

The New Youth Justice

The Crime and Disorder Act (1998) which 'hit the statute books in record time' (Pitts, 2001) identifies the determinants of juvenile crime in terms of 'risk conditions' such as lack of 'parental supervision, truancy, or lack of a stable home' (Muncie, 1999). In so doing, it side steps wider structural issues of material deprivation and poverty and focuses on crime prevention and early intervention into families and communities.

The Act represents 'a marked expansion of the legal means through which young people's behaviour can be circumscribed' (Muncie, 1999: p. 169). Individual and neighbourhood curfews have been introduced, and rationalised in terms of child protection as well as crime prevention (Muncie, 1999: p. 156). These have been seldom used, however. There are also *Anti-Social Behaviour Orders* (again these have been little used), and *Reparation Orders*. In addition, the police have been given more powers to deal with young people who truant from school. *Parenting Orders* have been introduced whereby parents can be penalised for the wrong doings of their children and fined £1000 if they do not make sure they attend school. As Muncie has pointed out, this is likely to exacerbate family tensions and may, ironically, lead to more young people becoming looked after.

The New Youth Justice, like the New Deal, is to be delivered locally through partnerships. Its focus is 'community safety'. Local authorities, the police, probation services, social services, youth services, statutory and voluntary sector organisations and local communities are enjoined to work together to reduce crime. The crime reduction element of the partnerships takes precedence over other concerns such as those of health (Barton, 1999) and it has been suggested that 'health and education authorities may have to incorporate new measures to meet the Act's requirements' (ISDD 1998: p. 3, cited in Barton, 1999: p. 474).

Youth Offender Teams (YOTs)

The Home Office established YOTs between April 1999 and March 2000. Every local authority with education and social services responsibilities was required to ensure that one or more YOT is established in the area they serve. YOTs are staffed by seconded personnel from the local authority, the police, the probation service, education and the health service. Each team has a steering group made up of senior representatives of the agencies involved and these steering groups link with:

- drug action teams
- community safety and crime reduction partnerships
- area child protection committees
- area criminal justice liaison committees
- social and economic regeneration groups

While welcoming the advent of YOTs, the youth justice practitioners organisation, the National Association for Youth Justice (NAYJ), has expressed strong reservations about their name. It argues that the term 'Youth Offender Teams' places too much emphasis upon 'young offenders', as opposed to young people who have committed offences. They believe that this could lead to the stigmatisation of those receiving the service. The association believes that they should be called 'Youth Development' or 'Youth Justice' teams.

YOTs co-ordinate the provision of local youth justice services. They may provide these services directly or co-ordinate their provision by other statutory, voluntary or private sector agencies. The minimum services they provide directly are:

- *Appropriate Adult* services.
- Assessment and intervention work in support of *Final Warnings* administered by the police.
- Bail information and support services.
- The placement of children and young people on transfer from the police and on remand from the court, in open or secure accommodation, remand fostering or approved lodgings.
- The preparation of Court reports.
- The co-ordination of provision of *Responsible Officers* for Child Safety Orders and Parenting Orders and undertaking such supervision work. This will require close liaison with Social Services.
- The supervision of children and young people sentenced to an Action Plan Order, Reparation Order, Supervision Order, Probation Order, Community Service Order or Combination Order. This may include drawing on programmes and activities provided outside the Youth Offending Team.
- Through-care and post-release supervision for young people sentenced to a Detention and Training Order or other custodial sentence.

A number of senior figures in the probation service have argued vociferously that they should be the lead agency in Youth Offender Teams because of the experience and expertise within the service. However, this overlooks the fact that the service has carried no responsibility for juveniles since 1964 and that, by the late 1990s, its principle responsibility was the supervision of high-tariff adult offenders.

The ways in which YOTs discharge their roles in practice can be inferred from the inter-agency youth justice panels currently in operation. Many of these operate 'Caution Plus' schemes of the type cited approvingly by the Audit Commission (1996) as a model for interventions which could accompany the *Final Warning*:

> These [inter-agency panels] *typically include representatives from the police, probation service, education, social services and education welfare. Occasionally, others such as the youth service and community groups may be represented on the panel. Ideally the panel members work as a team and make joint decisions and recommendations to the police who hold final responsibility for decision-making. It should also be recognised and accepted that decision-making can be difficult. This is because the different agencies involved have different roles and different primary responsibilities in respect of young people.*

> (NACRO, 1987: p. 5)

Effective inter-agency work requires the active collaboration of the statutory and voluntary agencies involved and the police. It should be monitored and evaluated rigorously in order to keep it on track. For that reason, participants need to be committed to shared goals, shared methods of data collection and the development and modification of professional and administrative practices as the strategy develops over time. Much of the research on inter-agency collaboration in the sphere of crime prevention suggests that:

- 'partnership' is not enough; it is the development of shared experience and a shared 'culture' which determines the effectiveness of such partnerships
- the active support and commitment of key figures at the head of the participating agencies is essential if they are to be more than talking shops, in which agencies simply attempt to discharge or displace their own agency responsibilities, or forums, in which the most powerful agency attempts to co-opt the others in order that it can discharge its pre-existing role more effectively. However, many inter-agency panels have surmounted these problems and the following mission statement of a panel in an inner-city borough gives a flavour of their ethos:

> The Walford Panel aims to prevent the continued involvement in crime of Walford children and young people aged between ten and seventeen who come to the attention of the police. The panel aims to ensure that children and young people recognise the seriousness of their behaviour and its actual and potential consequences for themselves and their victims. Nonetheless, the panel will operate in accordance with the UN Convention on the Rights of the Child, the Children Act (1989) and the Protocol on Standards in Youth Justice, issued by the Association of Directors of Social Services, which emphasise that the child or young person in trouble is also a 'child in need'. Thus the panel recognises that children and young people in trouble are growing and changing and that its work with them must have a 'developmental' orientation which promotes growth towards maturity and the development of high self-esteem. It is

therefore committed to responses to children and young people which build upon their strengths, rather than dwell upon their weaknesses, and strive to open up new opportunities for success rather than underlining past failures. Ultimately, the Panel is interested in what children and young people can become rather than what they have been in the past. As such, whenever and wherever possible, the panel will create interventions which are integrative rather than segregative, enabling young people to gain satisfaction from, and contribute creatively to, their homes, their schools and their neighbourhoods. The major administrative instrument whereby these goals are to be achieved will be the inter-agency panel.

For offenders who use drugs, specific schemes such as Arrest Referral Schemes and Drug Treatment and Testing Orders (DTTOs) have been introduced. Provision of drug services for young people, however, is still woefully inadequate and it has been argued that the impact of these schemes on young drug users has been 'negligible' as they have mostly been devised with male, adult offenders in mind (Newburn, 1999).

It has also been argued that there are a number of potential drawbacks to these schemes: they do not concern themselves with people's *motivations* for seeking treatment, instead people are sentenced to 'treatment' rather than to prison (Barton, 1999). This may make the drug counsellor's work more difficult.

Secondly, by 'fast-tracking' offenders into treatment, they take up places that those who decide to stop using drugs by their own volition would otherwise have had (Barton, 1999).

Thirdly, because of the requirements of multi-agency working, the drugs counsellor is required to share information about the young person with the police, social services and so on. This destroys the confidentiality of the relationship between the counsellor and client.

Fourthly, and perhaps most importantly, because of the different professional value bases from which Youth Offending Team members are drawn, there is a potential conflict between concern with *punishing* the young person and concern with the *welfare* of the young person (Barton, 1999). There is a danger that the criteria used to judge success in working with a young drug user will be 'the community-safety based success', or the 'reduction in crime', rather than the 'stabilisation of drug use' (Barton, 1999).

Career Opportunities: The Ones that Never Knock

(The Clash, 1980)

The 'New Deal' for young people links with the government's intention to 'fight crime and the causes of crime'. It is thought that young people who are integrated into the labour force are 'unlikely to become involved in criminal activity' (Holden, 1999: p. 530). The government has identified 'truancy and unemployment' as primary targets in its attempts to 'tackle the roots of juvenile crime' (Home Office, 1997, cited in Muncie 1999: p. 164). The 'New Deal' is different in some ways to work training schemes that have preceded it. It is delivered through local partnerships in which the private sector is more involved than it has previously been and it is based on a 'client-centred delivery model' (Theodore and Peck, 1999). However, the scheme is not as novel or as peerless as it may first appear. As Theodore and Peck (1999) argue, there is substantial convergence between the Job Seekers Allowance, introduced by the previous Conservative administration, and 'New Deal'. In particular, the latter promotes and extends the element of compulsion introduced by the Conservatives (Theodore and Peck, 1999; Tonge, 1999) and 'goes considerably further than the adoption of American workfare principles for claimants under 25' (Stepney *et al.*, 1999: p. 110). It has in fact been argued that 'New Deal' is 'marked by the extent of coercion involved rather than the job creation measures it has introduced' (Tonge, 1999). It has been described as a form of 'tough love', administered by a new breed of 'tough luvvies' (Jordan, 1999: p. 58). For young people a 'fifth option' of remaining on benefits or refusing 'offers of help' does not exist (DSS, 1998 cited in Stepney *et al.*, 1999: p. 110). Thus young people's rights to receive welfare benefits have been tied ever more closely to their obligation to work. Their participation in a fragmented, flexible and hyper-casualised labour market has been increased using coercive techniques such as the threat of withdrawal of benefits (Jordan, 1999).

The 'New Deal' provides young people who have been unemployed for more than six months with four options, each of which is accessed through a 'gateway'. The 'gateway' is a period, lasting up to 6 months, where young people are re-orientated to the labour market through intensive advice and counselling (Theodore and Peck, 1999). At the gateway, the options for young people are:

- to enter subsidised, or preferably unsubsidised, employment
- to work in the voluntary sector for three months and receive an appropriate qualification
- to join an 'environmental task force' or
- to enter training or education.

This last option is only open to those without minimal qualifications (NVQ level 2) (Theodore and Peck, 1999).

If young people decide on the employment option, the employer is subsidised by £60 per week for six months for employing them (Theodore and Peck, 1999). It is hoped that after this period the young person would be offered permanent employment although the employer is under no obligation to do so (Holden, 1999). Additionally, there is nothing to stop employers following one six-month period of subsidised employment with another (Working Brief, October, 1997, cited in Holden, 1999). If young people take the 'environmental task force' option, they receive their benefits plus £15 per week (Theodore and Peck, 1999). This 'amounts to £1.30 an hour for a 40 hour week' (Tonge, 1999).

The 'New Deal' initiative seeks solutions, through local partnerships between 'central, local and regional government, business, trade unions and voluntary or community organisations' to the national problem of unemployment: particularly youth unemployment (Theodore and Peck, 1999: p. 496). There are, however, considerable regional differences in the ways in which local partnerships are able to deliver the deal, particularly between regions of high and low unemployment. In fact, there are few examples of welfare to work schemes that 'have been effective in conditions of high unemployment and weak labour demand' (Theodore and Peck, 1999). It has therefore been suggested that the 'New Deal' for young people may be 'jeopardised by the geography of unemployment' (Turok and Webster, 1998, cited in Theodore and Peck, 1999).

Regardless of the geographical variations in the delivery and experience of 'New Deal' arrangements, all young people will experience its regulatory (and disempowering) effect. In terms of the young people who took part in this study, this may only serve to further undermine their attachment to the values and norms the government would require of them. Eroding the social rights of young people may only make it more likely that they will reject the obligations and responsibilities that increasingly accompany those rights (Dean and Melrose, 1996, 1997; Dean, 1997). 'Training without jobs' (Theodore and Peck, 1999) or insecure employment, where they are likely to be paid the minimum wage of £3.00 an hour if they are aged 18–21 and £3.20 an hour if they are 22 or over and receiving training, may not provide an incentive to stop using drugs.

Just as 'New Deal' has implications for the sorts of young people in this study, so other 'reforms' and 'initiatives' have impacted on the types of young people who took part:

- young people who have offended
- young people who have been excluded from school and
- young people who have been looked after.

Developments in the youth justice system, policies around school exclusions and looked after young people have particular implications for these groups. These are briefly explored next.

Putting it all into Practice

What has been said so far in this chapter demonstrates that the socio-economic and legal context makes the work of professionals with young people who have complex and overlapping problems, such as those who took part in this study, all the more difficult. Practitioners may even question the value of studies such as this in helping them in the task of understanding the issues involved, or indeed, how these may relate to their practice. The author hopes that one purpose this study serves is to confirm for practitioners what they know from their practice with vulnerable young people, that these young people face a range of interconnected and overlapping problems for which there is no 'quick fix' or overnight solution.

To add to these difficulties, we have seen that these young people, all of whom had similar experiences in terms of their offending, educational and looked after careers, engaged in drug use for different reasons. In responding to young people involved in drug use it is essential that practitioners build on existing knowledge about good practice with such young people: developing good relationships between young people and professionals involved in their care is fundamental. The views of the young people must be taken into account and careful assessment and planning to meet their care needs is essential.

> The question of a young person's motivations for using drugs is an important one to explore if appropriate interventions are to be suggested. Assuming homogeneity of need, misses the mark and prevents the development of appropriate responses. Successful approaches will require that the young person is viewed holistically and that their drug use is understood within the full context of their lives.

For example, if the young person appears to be seeking oblivion through drug use, then they need to be provided with opportunities for counselling so that they can explore, and hopefully, overcome the deeper problems of which their drug use is often a symptom. If, on the other hand, a young person is using drugs primarily in order to 'fit in' or to be accepted by their peer group, then providing them with opportunities in which they can establish positive peer associations will be important. An example of this is to offer sporting and leisure opportunities in which young people become engaged in peer networks that are less dangerous than those they appear to gravitate towards when left to their own devices. It has been found in previous work with vulnerable young people that peer interventions are something they value (Melrose *et al.*, 1999). Additionally or alternatively, such opportunities may be provided through peer mentoring and education schemes and by providing young people with opportunities for volunteering. The latter have been found to inform their vocational choices.

If a young person is using drugs because they are seeking 'thrills' or attempting to inject excitement into an otherwise mundane existence, then creative responses are required in order to provide young people with the excitement they feel they lack. It would be important for practitioners to explore with young people what other sources of excitement young people may value. Opportunities may be provided, for example, through activities that the young person considers to be 'on the edge'; that is, activities that stimulate their adrenaline may be valued.

It is also essential that practitioners take into account the circumstances and situations in which young people may be using drugs as well as the types of drugs they may be using as these may require different responses; recreational use for example will require a different response than chaotic use. A young person who is using heroin will require a different sort of intervention to a young person who is using cannabis. Similarly, a young person who is using drugs such as amphetamine on a daily basis will require a different response to one who is using it every month when they are going to raves. Above all, practitioners need to ensure that the young people with whom they work are appropriately educated about the risks attached to using particular drugs in particular ways and the risks attached to combining different drugs. Such education should be appropriate to the age and knowledge of the child and moreover, should be honest about the risks posed by the use of different drugs. As the Police Foundation report recently acknowledged, 'when young people know from their own experience that part of the message is exaggerated or untrue, there is a serious risk they will discount all the rest' (Bennetto, 2000). Creative forms, such as drama workshops or 'forum' theatre may be appropriate tools to employ to 'get the message across' to vulnerable young people. In 'forum theatre' after they have seen the action the audience are invited to see it again and to change the outcomes of the drama by intervening (Sheffield Theatres CYT, 2000).

Overall, the welfare of the child must remain paramount and a harm reduction approach to drug use should be adopted where this is appropriate. It is also obviously important that all agencies with whom the young person is in touch give consistent messages about drug use, that teachers, youth workers, social workers, juvenile justice workers and others should be singing from the same song sheet and all giving the young person the same message.

It is also important, when advising young people about the potential harm that may result from drug use, that those involved in working with and caring for them reinforce where appropriate and counter where necessary, the messages about drugs that young people have picked up through their own experience. Advice about using alcohol and cigarettes should also be included in any drugs education they receive. It may be too easy to overlook the more 'normalised' use of these intoxicants in favour of concentrating on illicit substances.

> Given the differences that were found between the young women and men to whom we spoke, there is an obvious need for drug education to address issues of sex-specific harm that may result from drug use. Drug education may also usefully explore the gender-specific meanings that attach to drug use and develop gender-specific messages about the consequences of drug use. Those providing services to young drug users should also be aware that the needs of young female drug users may be quite different to those of young male drug users.

When vulnerable young people who use drugs are the subject of youth justice, social service or educational service interventions, there is a need to ensure that they are not placed in situations where their vulnerability may escalate as this will only ensure that their risk of developing problems in relation to drug use will be increased.

There is still a great deal to do to extend voluntary and statutory drug services for young people as currently the level of provision for this group is underdeveloped. In view of this it is important that all professionals working with young people, and vulnerable young people in particular, develop a degree of drug literacy. Young people who are excluded from school, involved in offending or looked after will frequently first encounter professionals who are not experts in drug misuse and neither teachers, social workers nor probation officers should be expected to perform this role. The Youth Offending Teams, however, provide important opportunities for professionals to share expertise but this is unfortunately less true in other areas. Indeed, in relation to looked after young people, questions of health generally, and drug use in particular, have often been neglected.

Drug services that are developed to respond to the needs of young drug users would ideally be 'street-based', providing outreach and drop-in facilities. Previous research has shown that young people tend to respond better to these than to traditional forms of service delivery (Crosby and Barrett, 1999; Browne and Falshaw, 1998). Services should also be provided in confidence and where there is a need to break that confidence, or inform other agencies about the young person's drug use, the child or young person should be consulted and informed of this (Evans *et al.*, 1999).

> Practitioners need to take account of the individual circumstances of each child and determine when interventions are necessary and what **is** the appropriate response.

It is clear that there is a need for both 'joined-up-thinking' and 'joined-up-practice' in relation to young people and drugs generally and in relation to vulnerable young people and drug use in particular. It is to be hoped that this book will contribute to this thinking and will facilitate 'joined-up-practice' by those professionals who are concerned with the welfare and well-being of young people in contemporary Britain.

Case Study Examples of Life Histories

Here are two typical examples of the life histories of the young people who took part in the study which illustrates the complexity of their life experiences. These histories demonstrate that experiences other than offending, exclusion from school and being looked after in local authority care services render young people vulnerable to initiating drug use and to developing drug misuse problems.

'Beth'

Beth was seventeen when we met and living in a hostel in London. She had first become looked after between the ages of three and four because her father was in prison and her mother, a drug addict, found it difficult to cope. Beth was looked after again between the ages of seven and eight when her parents divorced. It was at this time that she first began to use alcohol, cigarettes, cannabis and volatile substances. After leaving care at eight, Beth returned to live with her mother while her brothers went to live with her father. At this age, Beth's mother used to take her shoplifting with her instead of sending her to school. She was first charged with an offence of shoplifting when she was ten and round about this time she stopped attending school completely. By eleven years of age Beth was drinking heavily and at this age was charged with an offence of defrauding a prescription, which she had done on behalf of her mother. At twelve, because she had stopped attending school, Beth was officially excluded. She continued shoplifting and at the age of fourteen began to use amphetamines regularly. When she was sixteen, Beth began to use cocaine and heroin intravenously on a daily basis. At this time she was regularly being raped by her uncle for whom she babysat. She told no-one about the abuse, but attempted suicide by jumping from a bridge. As a result of her attempted suicide Beth was admitted to hospital from where she was referred to a drug rehabilitation project. With the support of a youth justice worker and a social worker, she stopped using heroin and cocaine. At seventeen, Beth ran away to London. She had no means of supporting herself and was 'sleeping rough' and shoplifting. She got caught shoplifting and spent a week in Holloway prison. At the time of the interview, Beth was living in temporary accommodation in a hostel. She told us that since leaving the drug rehabilitation clinic she had only used cannabis. In the month before the interview, Beth had used alcohol, cigarettes and cannabis.

'Billy'

Billy's parents had divorced before he was four and his mother brought him up. When he was twelve, Billy was convicted of theft. At fourteen Billy began to use alcohol, was excluded from school for bad behaviour and shortly afterwards he became looked after because he was continually getting into trouble and his mother could not deal with him. He started smoking cigarettes at fifteen and also began to use cannabis and amphetamines. He continued to get into trouble with the police. At 16 Billy was using amphetamine daily and also at this time he began to use cocaine and crack. He used amphetamine daily for a period of one and half years and used crack daily for a period of a month and used cocaine occasionally for a year. Between the ages of twelve and seventeen, Billy served four spells in young offenders institutions for a few months each time. He was 17 and living in a hostel when we met and said he had only used cannabis, alcohol and cigarettes in the month before the interview.

Appendix 2

Average Age of First Use of all Substances Across all Groups

	Offended	Excluded	Looked After*	Offended and Excluded	Offended Excluded and Looked After	Excluded and Looked After**
Drugs	13.5	12.5	*	13.3	12.5	**
Alcohol	13	10.3	*	13.5	12	10
Tobacco	11.5	10.5	10	12.6	11.3	9.5
Volatile Substances	***	***	none	13.1	11.8	**

   * It was not possible to calculate averages for these substances because in the looked after group only one person had used drugs and alcohol

  ** It was not possible to calculate an average for these substances in this group because, of the two drug and volatile substance users, only one person gave the age at which they had begun to use these substances

*** In the offended group and the excluded group, only one person had used volatile substances, so it was not possible to calculate an average

Bibliography

Advisory Council on the Misuse of Drugs (ACMD) (1998). *Drug Misuse and the Environment.* London: The Stationary Office.

Anderson, B. (1991). *Imagined Communities.* London: Verso.

Andrews, K., and Jacobs, J. (1990). *Punishing the Poor: Poverty Under Thatcher.* Basingstoke: Macmillan.

Audit Commission (1996). *Misspent Youth: Young People and Crime.* Audit Commission.

Barclay, Sir P. (1995). *Inquiry into Income and Wealth*, Vol. 1. York: Joseph Rowntree Foundation.

Barton, A. (1999). Sentenced to Treatment? Criminal Justice Orders and the Health Service. *Critical Social Policy*, 19(4): 61.

Becker, H. (1963). *Outsiders: Studies in the Sociology of Deviance.* New York: NY Free Press.

Bennett, T. (1998). *Drug Testing Arrestees. Home Office Research Findings*, No. 70. London: Home Office.

Bennetto, J. (2000). Inquiry Calls for Soft Line on Hard Drugs: But Blair Says No. *The Independent*, March 29th.

Berridge, D. and Brodie, I. (1998). *Children's Homes Revisited.* London: Jessica Kingsley.

Blackman, S. (1997). Deconstructing a Giro: A Critical and Ethnographic Study of the Youth 'Underclass'. In MacDonald, R. (Ed.). *Youth, 'the Underclass' and Social Exclusion.* London: Routledge.

Blom, M., and van den Berg, T. (1989). A Typology of the Life and Work Styles of 'Heroin Prostitutes': From Male Career Model to a Feminised Career Model. In Cain, M. (Ed.). *Growing Up Good: Policing the Behaviour of Girls in Europe.* London: Sage.

Bloomfield, R., and Kerr, J. (2000). Matters of Substance. *Time Out*, April 12th–19th: 18–9

Bourgois, P. (1996). *In Search of Respect: Selling Crack in El Barrio.* Cambridge: Cambridge University Press.

Bradshaw, J. (1990). *Child Poverty and Deprivation in the UK.* London: National Children's Bureau.

Breeze, E. (1985). *Women and Drinking: An Enquiry Carried out on Behalf of the Department of Health and Social Security.* London: HMSO.

British Youth Council (1992). *The Time of Your Life? The Truth About Being Young in 1990s Britain.* London: British Youth Council.

Browne, K., and Falshaw, L. (1998). Street Children in the UK: A Case of Abuse and Neglect. *Child Abuse Review*, 7: 241–53.

Burroughs, W. (1977). *Junky.* London: Penguin Books.

Burton, P., Forrest, R., and Stewart, M. (1989). *Growing Up and Leaving Home.* Dublin: European Foundation for the Improvement of Living and Working Conditions.

Cabinet Office (1998). *Tackling Drugs: Government Action.* London: Cabinet Office.

Carter, H. (1998). 1 in 10 Workers Test Positive for Drugs. *The Guardian*, November 2nd.

Clash, The (1980). Career Opportunities. *Sandinista!* CBS Music.

Cohen, S. (1973). *Folk Devils and Moral Panics.* St. Albans: Paladin.

Coles, B. (1986). Gonna Tear your Playhouse Down: Towards Reconstructing the Sociology of Youth. *Social Science Teacher*, 15(3): 78–80.

Coles, B. (1995). *Youth and Social Policy: Youth Citizenship and Young Careers.* London.

Coles, B., and Craig, G. (1999). Excluded Youth and the Growth of Begging. In Dean, H. (Ed.). *Begging Questions: Street Level Economic Activity and Social Policy Failure.* Bristol: The Policy Press.

Collison, M. (1996). In Search of the High Life: Drugs, Crime, Masculinities and Consumption. *British Journal of Criminology*, 36(3): 428–44.

Coyle, D., and Grice, A. (2000). Poverty Gap Widens Under Blair. *The Independent*, April 13th.

Craine, S. (1997). The 'Black Magic Roundabout': Cyclical Transitions, Social Exclusion and Alternative Careers. In MacDonald, R. (Ed.). Op. cit.

Crosby, S., and Barrett, D. (1999). Poverty, Drugs and Youth Prostitution: A Case Study of Service Providers' Practical Responses. In Marlow, A., and Pearson, G. (Eds.). *Young People, Drugs and Community Safety.* Lyme Regis: Russell House Publishing.

Dally, A. (1999). Anomalies and Mysteries in the 'War on Drugs'. In Porter, R., and Teich, M. (Eds.). *Drugs and Narcotics in History.* Cambridge: Cambridge University Press.

Davis, M., with Ruddick, S. (1988). Los Angeles: Civil Liberties between the Hammer and the Rock. *New Left Review*, No. 170.

Davison, J. (1997). *Gangsta.* London: Vision Paperbacks a division of Satin Publications Limited.

Dean, H. (1997). Underclassed or Undermined? Young People and Social Citizenship. In MacDonald, R. (Ed.). Op. cit.

Dean, H., and Gale, K. (1999). Begging and the Contradictions of Citizenship. In Dean, H. (Ed.). Op. cit.

Dean, H., and Melrose, M. (1996). Unravelling Citizenship: The Significance of Social Security Benefit Fraud. *Critical Social Policy*, 48: 16(3).

Dean, H., and Melrose, M. (1997). Manageable Discord: Fraud and Resistance in the Social Security System. *Social Policy and Administration*, 32: 2.

Dean, H., and Melrose, M. (1999). Easy Pickings or Hard Profession? In Dean, H. (Ed.) Op. cit.

Dean, H., and Taylor-Gooby, P. (1994). *Dependency Culture: The Explosion of a Myth*. Hemel Hempstead: Harvester Wheatsheaf.

Dean, H., with Melrose, M. (1998). *Poverty, Riches and Social Citizenship*. Basingstoke: Macmillan.

Denton, B., and O'Malley, P. (1999). Gender, Trust and Business: Women Drug Dealers in the Illicit Economy. *British Journal of Criminology*, 39; 4 (Special Issue): 513–30

Department for Education and Employment (1999). *Social Exclusion: Pupil Support*. London: The Stationary Office.

Department for Education and Employment/Department of Health (1999). *Draft Guidance on the Education of Children Looked After by Local Authorities*. London: Department for Education and Employment/Department of Health.

Department of Health (1996). *Focus on Teenagers*. London: HMSO.

Department of Health (1998a). *Caring for Children Away from Home: Messages from Research*. Chichester: John Wiley and Sons.

Department of Health (1998b). *Quality Protects: Framework for Action*. London: Department of Health.

Dorn, N., and South, N. (Eds.) (1987). *A Land Fit for Heroin?* Basingstoke: Macmillan.

Douglas, A., and Gilroy, R. (1994). Young Women and Homelessness. In Gilroy, R., and Woods, R. (Eds.). *Housing Women*. London: Routledge,

Dutton, B. (1986). *The Media*. New York: Longman Inc.

Edmunds, M., May, T., Hearnden, I., and Hough, M. (1998). *Arrest Referral: Emerging Lessons from Research*. Drug Prevention Initiative, Paper 23. London: Home Office,

Edwards, S. (1998). Abused and Exploited—Young Girls in Prostitution: A Consideration of the Legal Issues. In *Whose Daughter Next? Children Abused Through Prostitution*. Essex: Barnardo's.

Elliot, L., Denny, C., and White, M. (2000). Poverty Gap Hits Labour Boasts. *The Guardian*, July 14th.

Ettorre, E. (1992). *Women and Substance Use*. Basingstoke: Macmillan.

Evans, K., Britton, J., Farrant, F., and Dale-Perrera, A. (1999). *Assessing Local Need: Drug Interventions for Vulnerable Young People*. The Good Practice Unit for Young People and Drug Misuse, SCODA.

Farmer, E., and Pollock, S. (1998). Sexually Abused and Abusing Children in Substitute Care. In *Caring for Children Away from Home: Messages from Research*. Department of Health. Chichester: John Wiley and Sons.

France, A. (1996). Youth and Citizenship in the 1990s. *Youth and Policy*, 53: 28–54.

Garrett, P. (1999). Producing the Moral Citizen: The Looking After Children System and the Regulation of Children and Young People in Public Care. *Critical Social Policy*, 19(3): 60.

Graham, J., and Bowling, B. (1995). *Young People and Crime.* Home Office Research Study No. 145. London: Home Office.

Gutzke, D. (1994). Gender, Class and Public Drinking in Britain during the First World War. *Social History*, Vol. XXVII; No. 54: November.

Hammersley, R., Ditton, J., Smith, I., and Short, E. (1999). Patterns of Ecstasy Use by Drug Users. *The British Journal of Criminology*, 39; 4 (Special Issue – Drugs at the End of the Century): 625–47.

Health Advisory Service (HAS) (1996). *Children and Young People: Substance Misuse Services: The Substance of Young Needs.* London: HMSO.

Hellawell, K. (1998/99). *The United Kingdom Anti-drugs Co-ordinator, First Annual Report and National Plan.* London: The Cabinet Office.

Henderson, S. (1999). Drugs and Culture: The Question of Gender. In South, N. (Ed.). *Drugs, Cultures, Controls and Everyday Life.* London: Sage.

Hills, J. (1995). *Inquiry into Income and Wealth*, Vol. 2. York: Joseph Rowntree Foundation.

Holden, C. (1999). Globalisation, Social Exclusion and Labour's New Work Ethic. *Critical Social Policy*, 61; 19(4): 529–38.

Holloway, S.W.F. (1998). The Regulation of the Supply of Drugs in Britain before 1868. In Porter, R., and Teich, M. (Eds.). Op. cit.

Hough, M. (1996). *Drug Misuse and the Criminal Justice System: A Review of the Literature.* Home Office Drugs Prevention Initiative, Paper 15. London: Home Office.

Hughes, K., MacKintosh, A.M., Hastings, G., Wheeler, C., Watson, J., and Inglis, J. (1997). Alcohol and Designer Drinks: Quantitative and Qualitative Study. *British Medical Journal*, 314: February.

Hutson, S., and Liddiard, M. (1994). *Youth Homelessness.* Basingstoke: Macmillan.

Jones, G. (1997). Youth Homelessness and the 'Underclass'. In MacDonald, R. (Ed.).Op. cit.

Jordan, B. (1996). *A Theory of Poverty and Social Exclusion.* Cambridge: Polity Press.

Jordan, B. (1999). Begging: the Global Context and International Comparisons. In Dean, H. (Ed.). Op. cit.

Joseph Rowntree Foundation (JRF) (1998). *Findings: Monitoring Poverty and Social Exclusion.* York: Joseph Rowntree Foundation.

Kohn, M. (1999). Cocaine Girls: Sex, Drugs and Modernity in London During and After the First World War. In Gootenberg, P. (Ed.). *Cocaine: Global Histories.* London: Routledge.

Kumar, V. (1993). *Poverty and Inequality in the UK: The Effects on Children.* London: National Children's Bureau.

Levitas, R. (1999). Defining and Measuring Social Exclusion: A Critical Overview of Current Proposals. *Radical Statistics*, 71: Summer.

Lloyd, B., Lucas, K., Holland, J., McGrellis, S., and Arnold, S. (1998). *Smoking in Adolescence.* London: Routledge.

MacDonald, R. (1997a). Dangerous Youth and the Dangerous Class. In MacDonald, R. (Ed.). Op. cit.

Macey, D. (1993). *The Lives of Michael Foucault.* London: Vintage.

Maguire, M., and Maguire, S. (1997). Young People and the Labour Market. In MacDonald, R. (Ed.). Op. cit.

Maher, L. (1995). In the Name of Love: Women and Initiation to Illicit Drugs. In Emerson-Dobash, R., Dobash, R.P., and Noakes, L. (Eds.). *Gender and Crime.* Cardiff: University of Wales.

Martin, T., Hayden, C., Turner, D., and Ramsell, K. (1999). *Out of School and into Trouble? Exclusion from School and Persistent Young Offenders.* A joint publication by the Social Services Research and Information Unit, University of Portsmouth and Hampshire Constabulary.

Matthee, R. (1999). Exotic Substances: The Introduction and Global Spread of Tobacco, Coffee, Coca, Tea and Distilled Liquor, Sixteenth to Eighteenth Centuries. In Porter, R., and Teich, M. (Eds.). Op. cit.

May, T., Edmunds, M., Hough, M., with Harevy. C. (2000). *Street Business: The Links Between Sex and Drug Markets.* Police Research Series, Paper 118. London: Home Office.

McCallum, T. (1998). *Drug Use by Young Females.* Health Education Unit, University of Sydney.

McLaughlin, E., and Glendenning, C. (1994). Paying for Care in Europe: Is There a Feminist Approach? In Hantrais, L., and Mangen, S. (Eds.). *Family Policy and the Welfare of Women.* University of Loughborough, Cross-national research papers.

Measham, F., Parker, H., and Aldridge, J. (1998). *Starting, Switching, Slowing and Stopping. Report for the Drug Prevention Initiative Integrated Programme.* London: The Home Office.

Melrose, M. (2000). Globalisation and Child Prostitution in Britain in the 1990s. Paper presented at *The Globalisation of Sexual Exploitation Conference*, Institute of Commonwealth Studies, London, July 10th.

Melrose, M., and Brodie, I. (1999). Developing Solutions for Young People Involved in Prostitution. Paper presented at the *Fourth International Conference on the Rights of the Child*, Quebec, Canada, October.

Melrose, M., Barrett, D., and Brodie, I. (1999). *One Way Street? Retrospectives on Childhood Prostitution.* London: The Children's Society.

Merchant, J., and MacDonald, R. (1994). Youth and the Rave Culture, Ecstasy and Health. *Youth and Policy*, 45.

Morley, D. (1991). Where the Global Meets the Local: Notes from the Sitting Room. *Screen*, 32(1):1–16.

Muncie, J. (1999). Institutionalised Intolerance: Youth Justice and the 1998 Crime and Disorder Act. *Critical Social Policy*, 59; 19(2): 147–76.

Murji, K. (1999). White Lines: Culture, 'Race' and Drugs. In South. N. (Ed.). Op. cit.

Murray, C. (1990). *The Emerging British Underclass.* London: Institute of Economic Affairs.

National Strategy for Neighbourhood Renewal (2000). *Report of the Policy Action Team 12: Young People.* London: The Stationary Office.

Newburn, T. (1999). Drug Prevention and Youth Justice: Issues of Philosophy, Practice and Policy. *British Journal Of Criminology*, 39: 4 (Special Issue).

Norman, E. (1994). Personal Factors Related to Substance Misuse: Risk Abatement and/or Resiliency Enhancement? In Gullota, T., and Montemayor, R. (Eds.). *Substance Misuse in Adolescence.* California: Sage.

O'Neill, M., Goode, N., and Hopkins, K. (1995). Juvenile Prostitution: The Experience of Young Women in Residential Care. *Childright*, 113: 14–6.

OFSTED (1996). *Exclusions from Secondary School 1995–96.* London: HMSO.

Oppenheimer, E. (1989). Young Female Drug Misusers: Towards an Appropriate Policy. In Cain, M. (Ed.). *Growing Up Good: Policing the Behaviour of Girls in Europe.* London: Sage.

Otero-Lopez, J.M., Luengo-Martin, A., Miron-Redondo, L., Carillo-de-la-Pena, M.T., and Romero-Trinanes, E. (1994). An Empirical Study of the Relations Between Drug Abuse and Delinquency Among Adolescents. *British Journal of Criminology*, 34; 4: 459–78.

Parascandola, J. (1998). The Drug Habit: The Association of the Word 'Drug' with Abuse in American History. In Porter, R., and Teich, M. (Eds.). Op. cit.

Parker, H. (1996). Young Adult Offenders, Alcohol and Criminological Cul-de-Sacs/ *British Journal of Criminology*, 36; 2:282–98.

Parker, H., Aldridge, J., and Measham, F. (1998). *Illegal Leisure: The Normalisation of Adolescent Drug Use.* London: Routledge.

Parker, H., Measham, F., and Aldridge, J. (1995). *Drugs Futures: Changing Patterns of Drug Use Amongst English Youth.* London: Institute for the Study of Drug Dependence.

Parssinen, T. (1983). *Secret Passions, Secret Remedies: Narcotic Drugs in British Society 1820–1930.* Manchester: Manchester University Press.

Pearson, G. (1987). Social Deprivation, Unemployment and Patterns of Heroin Use. In Dorn, N., and South, N. (Eds.). *A Land Fit for Heroin? Drug Policies, Prevention and Practice.* Basingstoke: Macmillan.

Pearson, G. (1999). Drugs at the End of the Century. Editorial introduction, *British Journal of Criminology*, 39; 4: 477–87.

Pettiway, L. (1997). *Workin' it: Women Living Through Drugs and Crime.* Philadelphia: Temple University Press.

Pitts, J. (1997). Causes of Youth Prostitution. In Barrett, D. (Ed.). *Child Prostitution in Britain: Dilemmas and Practical Responses.* London: The Children's Society.

Pitts, J. (1999). *Working with Young Offenders*. Basingstoke: Macmillan.

Pitts, J. (2001). *The New Politics of Youth Justice: Discipline or Solidarity?* Basingstoke: Palgrave.

President of the Council (1998). *Tackling Drugs to Build a Better Britain: The Government's Ten Year Strategy for Tackling Drugs Misuse*, Cm. 3945: April.

Ramsay, M. (1999). New Perspectives on Drug Surveys: Comments on Articles by Sheila Gore and Ziggy Macdonald. *British Journal of Criminology*, 39: 4 (Special Issue).

Rayner, J. (2000). Drugs Tsar Defies Spin Machine. *The Observer*, February 6th.

Robson, P. (1999). *Forbidden Drugs* (2nd edn.). Oxford: Oxford University Press.

Roche, J., and Tucker, S. (1997). *Youth in Society: Contemporary Theory, Policy and Practice*. London: Sage.

Ruggerio, V. (1999). Drugs as a Password and the Law as a Drug: Discussing the Legalisation of Illicit Substances. In South. N. (Ed.). Op. cit.

Ruggerio, V., and South, N. (1997). The Late Modern City as Bazaar: Drug Markets, Illegal Enterprise and the 'Barricades'. *British Journal of Sociology*, 48; 1: 54–70.

Scott, J. (1994). *Poverty and Wealth: Citizenship, Deprivation and Privilege*. Essex: Longman.

Shapiro, H. (1999). Dances with Drugs: Pop Music, Drugs and Youth Culture. In South, N. (Ed.). Op. cit.

Sheffield Theatres CYT (2000). *Not Exactly an Angel*. The Brady Centre, Tower Hamlets, London, 1st June.

Shiner, M., and Newburn, T. (1999). Taking Tea with Noel: The Place and Meaning of Drug Use in Everyday Life. In South, N. (Ed.). Op. cit.

Shiner, M., and Newburn, T. (1997). Definitely, Maybe Not? The Normalisation of Recreational Drug Use Amongst Young People. *Sociology*, 31; 3: 511–29.

Sidorenko-Stephenson, S. (1999). Moscow Street Children and Emerging Urban Marginality. Paper presented to panel on *Youth and Cultural Globalisation in Post-Soviet Russia, BASEES Conference*, Fitzwilliam College, Cambridge March 27th–29th.

Sinclair, I., and Gibbs, I. (1998). *Children's Homes: A Study in Diversity*. Chichester: Wiley.

Social Exclusion Unit (1998). *Truancy and School Exclusions: Report by the Social Exclusion Unit*, Cm. 3957. London: Stationary Office.

South, N. (1997). Drugs: Use, Crime and Control. In Maguire, M., Morgan, R., and Reiner, R. (Eds.). *The Oxford Handbook of Criminology* (2nd edn.). Oxford: Clarendon Press.

South, N. (1999). Debating Drugs and Everyday Life: Normalisation, Prohibition and 'Otherness'. In South, N. (Ed.). Op. cit.

Standing Conference on Drug Abuse (SCODA) (1997). *Drug-related Early Interventions: Developing Services for Young People and Families*. London: Standing Conference on Drug Abuse, The Good Practice Unit for Young People and Drug Misuse.

Stepney, P., Lynch, R., and Jordan, B. (1999). Poverty, Exclusion and New Labour. *Critical Social Policy*, 58; 19(1): 109–28.

Stimson, G. (1987). The War on Heroin: British Policy and the International Trade in Illicit Drugs. In Dorn, N., and South, N. (Eds.). Op cit.

Taylor, P. (1984). *The Smoke Ring: Tobacco, Money and Multi-national Politics.* London: Sphere Books.

Theodore, N., and Peck, J. (1999). Welfare-to-Work: National Problems, Local Solutions? *Critical Social Policy*, 61; 19(4): 485–510.

Tonge, J. (1999). New Packaging, Old Deal? Labour and Employment Policy Innovation. *Critical Social Policy*, 19(2): 59.

Townsend, P. (1996). *A Poor Future.* London: Lemos and Crane.

Travis, A. (2000). Heroin: Abusers Start at 15. *The Guardian*, April 5th.

Triseliotis, J., Borland, M., Hill, M., and Lambert, L. (1995). *Teenagers and the Social Work Services.* London: HMSO.

Turnbull, P., Webster, R., and Stillwell, G. (1996). *'Get it While You Can': An Evaluation of an Early Intervention Project for Arrestees with Alcohol and Drug Problems.* Drugs Prevention Initiative Home Office Paper 9. London: Home Office.

Tyler, A. (1995). *Street Drugs: The Facts Explained, the Myths Exploded* (3rd edn.). London: Hodder and Stoughton.

Utting, Sir W. (1997). *People Like Us: The Report of the Review of the Safeguards for Children Living Away from Home.* London: The Stationary Office.

Wade, J., Biehal, N., Clayden, J., and Stein, M. (1998). Going Missing: Young People Absent from Care. In Dartington Social Research Unit, Department of Health. *Caring for Children Away from Home.* Chichester: John Wiley and Sons.

Whiteside, N. (1995). Employment Policy: A Chronicle of Decline? In Gladstone, D. (Ed.). *British Social Welfare: Past, Present and Future.* London: UCL Press.

Williamson, H. (1997). Status Zero Youth and the 'Underclass', Some Considerations. In MacDonald, R. (Ed.). Op. cit.

Wyatt, G.E., Newcomb, M., and Riederle, M. (1993). *Sexual Abuse and Consensual Sex: Women's Developmental Patterns and Outcomes.* California: Sage.